Row Your Own Boat

Chart your own course
Master your own life
Take control of your future
and
Row Your Own Boat!

Sharon Cleveley and Viv Walker

ISBN: 978-1-3999-0243-4

ROW YOUR OWN BOAT DISCLAIMER

The authors (Sharon Cleveley and Vivianne Walker) state that this book has been written as an informative, guiding, and educational resource for personal development assistance in relation to the subjects addressed.

The advice and strategies contained in this book may not be suitable for every person or situation, so this book is sold with the understanding that the authors are not engaged in offering medical, legal, or other professional advice or services. If any reader requires professional assistance, the services of a competent person should be sought. Readers should consult their medical practitioner before changing, stopping, or starting any medical treatment.

The authors disclaim any liability for any damages arising directly or indirectly from the use or misuse of the information contained in this book.

The authors also state that any references to other individuals, organisations, or websites does not mean that they endorse the information the individual, organisation, or website may provide or recommendations they or it may make. Furthermore, readers should be aware that websites listed in this book may have changed or disappeared between the time of writing and the time of reading.

www.rowyourownboat.co.uk

Dedication

This book is dedicated to those of you

who are ready to

Row Your Own Boat,

Captain your own ship,

and become

Master of your own destiny.

Acknowledgements

Thank you to our families and friends who supported and encouraged us as we produced this book.

A special thank you also goes to those who have patiently listened to us, read our draft versions, offered advice and suggestions and were there for us when we needed them.

A final thank you goes to our editor, Jo Lavender (www.inkpotediting.co.uk) for her help in getting this book into shape.

Contents

PREFACE

Sharon and I met in the early 1990s when we were both working as trainers and workplace assessors for the same company. We delivered government-funded training programs aimed at getting people into work. The unemployment rate in the UK at that time was around 10% (well over 2 million), so we were never short of clients and we dealt with people of all ages, from 16-year-old school leavers who could barely spell their own names to those who had become unemployed in their late 50s or early 60s.

Based in Birmingham, the second-largest city in the UK, our clients were from all backgrounds, religions, and ethnicities, and they had diverse and sometimes challenging attitudes. Despite their outward differences, many of our clients did have a few things in common: most struggled financially, and as their bank balances dwindled, some fell into debt and had their homes or other items repossessed. For a despondent few, relationships ended and families separated under the strain. Mentally, they all suffered. They had lost their confidence; their self-esteem had vanished; and a sense of hopelessness had engulfed them.

With so many people unemployed, how could they get a job?

Sharon and I both taught Job Search skills, along with 'soft' skills such as assertiveness, problem-solving, confidence and self-esteem building, time management, team working, etc. I also used to teach typing and IT software use, along with all aspects of Business Administration work, and Sharon taught Administration, Customer Service, and Management Skills. She later moved on to designing and running Modern Apprenticeships programs for the under 25s.

I am proud to say that we made a difference to many people's lives. We managed to get most of the people who wanted to work into work. The sense of satisfaction we used to feel when helping others was phenomenal. These people didn't just get a job – we gave them the help they needed to get their whole lives back!

A few years ago, when I moved out of Birmingham, I left my training career behind but, having had the idea for this book years earlier, I carried on collecting thoughts and jotting down notes for it.

In 2020, as COVID-19 hit hard, I shared my thoughts and a few ideas for this book with Sharon, knowing that without her valuable input I would not be able to complete it. I was delighted that she thought it was a good idea and offered to join me in this journey.

Sharon has had more experience delivering training than me and, having had her share of life's ups and downs, she was also keen to help people by sharing her ways of coping with and moving past the bad stuff. Without her *'Row Your Own Boat'* would not have happened so I am beyond grateful that I have had such a great crew mate to make this journey with.

Between us, we have decades of know-how and experience which we have drawn on to produce this new way of looking at life.

In this book, you'll be getting advice from both of us and we hope that you'll find a few ideas to suit you, which you can use to improve your life's journey.

Viv Walker

Introduction

Row, row, row your boat,

Gently down the stream,

Merrily, merrily, merrily, merrily

Life is but a dream.

Let's start this journey together by acknowledging the fact that you've picked up this book because you're not happy with something about your life at the moment.

We know that a lot of self-help books work by encouraging you to be mega-successful and helping you to do super-duper things:

Do you want to be a successful business owner? A millionaire? A perfect partner or parent? Follow the practices of highly successful people to rise above or out of the life you have now?

If you want to do one or two of those things, fair enough; you should go for it – but this may not be the right book for you.

This book is for people who just know that something is 'off.'

You might not know what it is, but as you think about your life's journey to date, you simply know that there's something wrong or something lacking. Whatever it is (and it could be anything, large or small), you know that there's something about your life, a part of your day-to-day existence, that could be better.

You might be able to pinpoint a certain thing and say, 'I need to change that', or you might simply have the nagging thought that one day you'd like to be, or to do, something different. You may not feel a need to become massively successful, but you want to do, or have, something more in your life than you have right now.

There could be many reasons why you feel unsettled about where you are currently:

- Perhaps your relationships aren't giving you what you need to thrive?
- Are you unhappy with your current employment (or lack of it)?

- Maybe your cash flow or money management needs attention?
- Could your health and fitness be better?
- Do you feel you need to be more confident or outgoing?

You may be acutely aware of what you would like (or need) to change and how you could go about it, or you might simply have a general feeling that something's not right.

Are you happy?

We don't mean 'jumping up and down with joy and leaping out of bed with a song in your heart every morning' happy. We mean are you happy with your life as it is right now?

We're guessing the answer is 'no,' or, more likely, while you may not be acutely miserable, you know that you're not as satisfied or contented with your life as you'd like to be.

Perhaps you feel that you're simply plodding along through life, doing the right things, making the right noises, and pleasing the right people...

But is that enough?

Where is your contentment?

Where is your hope?

Where is your joy?

Where is the sense of achievement you thought you'd have by now?

Do you feel that time is slipping away but you still have goals and dreams you haven't achieved?

Where is the person you used to think you'd be by now?

Are you living your best life?

If the answer is an emphatic 'NO', what happened?

Maybe you've been feeling this way for a while, or maybe it's only recently crept up on you?

But at this moment, you absolutely know that something's 'off.'

You are aware that something needs to change to make you think and feel better about where you are.

But what?

And more importantly…

How?

This is where ***Row Your Own Boat*** can help.

Whether you only need to achieve a minor target (learn to speak French or plan your meals better) or you have to do something radical (get a divorce, change jobs, train to be an astronaut), you'll find the help you need right here.

In this book, you'll find a new way of looking at your life, a way of examining it in a different light and from different angles.

We'll start with looking back at your journey to date – your personal history. This will include the good things as well as the issues, traumas, and the other negative 'stuff' you've had to deal with.

We'll also look at the achievements you've made along the way. In essence, we'll cover everything which has shaped the person you are today.

Then we'll look at what you ***really*** want to do from now on.

With our help, you'll be able to identify how you want to live, what you want to do, who you want to be with, and where you want to go.

After that, you can look at your future and make plans to achieve the things you want to achieve.

For this, we're going to do a bit of imagining. It's not a new idea, but we believe this could give you a different way to look at and manage your life from now on…

Imagine that you are living your whole life in a boat.

It could be a tiny canoe, a rowing boat, a speedboat, a yacht, a cruiser, or any other boat you would like to imagine yourself being in.

To start with, we suggest that you think of your boat as a small rowing boat.

Why a rowing boat?

We prefer this image because a rowing boat is powered by you. You have total control; you can row in any direction you want, and you're not necessarily dependent on anyone else.

Take a moment and try, if you can, to imagine that everyone in the world is living their life in their own rowing boat.

Some boats are tied together in family groups or other bubbles, but each person spends most of their time in their own boat.

When we are born, we are delivered into our mother's boat. If we are lucky, we'll stay in this vessel with her (or another grown-up) for a long time and our childhood will be spent in the safety of an adult's boat. The adult will plot the course and protect us from the waves and storms. They will feed us, clothe us, make most of the decisions for us, and do ***all*** of the rowing.

As we grow and become more self-aware, we realise that we each have our own little boat, but the adults have it tied safely to the back of theirs. We can sit in it, but they keep us close; they navigate the route and constantly protect us. Other significant people may be in boats all around us, such as siblings and other relatives, neighbours, friends, teachers – all forming a flotilla of tiny boats.

Later on, as we grow, we are allowed a little more rope so that we can practice rowing our own boat, safe in the knowledge that we're still attached to our protectors, who can reel us in and help us whenever we need it.

We know that the people around us are there for us when we need them.

When we're fully grown, most of us cut the rope and start to row on our own, but still keep our protectors in sight, and often follow their course.

We might then look around and decide whether we want to carry on travelling alongside the people we know, or whether we want to go somewhere else. If we want to go elsewhere, we have to decide how we're going to get there and set off alone. However...

For most of us, life is rarely that simple.

Sometimes we just cannot decide where we want to go to, or how to plot the route to get there.

If we do have a route planned, we may be tossed and battered by stormy seas.

Sometimes, we'll veer off course and end up lost and alone in a vast sea of emptiness.

We may encounter pirates and brigands, or we could discover stowaways having a free ride at our expense. Some people may be hanging on to the side of the boat, weighing us down, while others have tied a rope from their boat to the back of ours, helping themselves to a free tow.

Perhaps we don't mind helping some of these people, but the added weight can make it more and more difficult for us to keep rowing along our chosen course.

There may also be times when we become ill, or we are simply too tired to row our boats any longer.

Storms rise; we are tossed and turned with the waves. In the tempest, the boat may become waterlogged or spring a leak; it might even begin to sink, and we may fear drowning.

If we're lucky, we may find help; someone may offer us a rope or let us ride in the back of their boat, giving us a rest as they take us to a safe haven, perhaps a dry dock where we can get help and repairs.

Unfortunately, most of us just have to manage as best we can, bailing out the water, plugging the holes, and hanging on for dear life until the storms have passed, all while hoping that we'll eventually be able to rest and recover.

Too proud or too ashamed to ask for help, some of us never learn how to row our own boats successfully.

Some people choose to stay in the first safe harbour they reach, too scared to risk the journey that they would like to make.

Other people, when they do venture out to sea, struggle to navigate their plotted course. Some never learn how to avoid the storms, or how to survive them and make repairs, until one day they find that they have fallen overboard and have the fight of their lives to stay afloat.

Let's remember the 'Row, row, row, your boat' nursery rhyme, in which *'Life is just a dream.'* Life, remember, is something that you should be able to enjoy, at least most of the time.

It is a shame that few of us can sit back in our little boats, relax, and enjoy the journey.

Life should not, and does not have to be a hard slog all the time.
But how many of us are ***actually*** happy or content?

How many of us can steer our boats in the right direction, no matter what the weather is doing, no matter where the current is trying to take us?

How many of us will get to our chosen destination with our boats intact and both hands still on the oars?

Many of us will need physical or mental support at some point in our voyage, and if we can find and accept this assistance, we can keep going and reach the destination we are aiming for, and enjoy the journey too.

In this book, we'll be offering help, advice, and guidance to show you how to assess and improve your boat, how to plot a course you actually want to follow, and how to experience a better journey across your ocean from now on.

We'll cover aspects such as sitting safely in your harbour, launching out to open sea, and how to cope with storms, pirates, and other perils on the way.

Most of us drift through life on whatever currents carry us along, simply going with the flow. While we might not be miserable, we are often aware that we are not as happy as we could be.

We just don't know how to step back and look at ourselves from a different angle or take on a new approach to life.

It's only when you stop and look, ***really look,*** *that you can see what's been missing or what's holding you back from the happiness you deserve.*

By giving you tips and techniques we have used over the years, we hope to offer you a new, helpful way of looking at your life, so you can become the best captain of your own boat that you can be.

This is your boat and your journey.

To get maximum value from this book, we advise that you work through each chapter in order (although you can pick and choose sections that you think will help you along your way and ignore the rest if you want to).

Throughout the book there are activities which you can complete, with spaces for your notes, but for those of you who don't want to write in your copy of the book, we have a resource pack of worksheets available for you to print, simply email us at info@rowyourownboat.co.uk to request a copy.

Note from Viv

Now in my sixties, I've survived many personal storms and terrible tempests. I occasionally arrived at a safe haven where I enjoyed happiness for a while, but I've also been a castaway, washed ashore, and stranded in places I didn't want to be. My boat has sprung leaks, and been broken and scuppered more times than I care to admit. Looking back, I can see that I learned to roll with the waves and hang on, sometimes by my fingernails, through the bad times.

I was deaf until I was eight years old. Two operations gave me back most of my hearing. I was illegitimate at a time when it wasn't acceptable in society and was shamed because of it. My mentally unstable mother left me to be raised by my grandparents. Although she was the cause of many dramas over the years, we did become friends in later life.

My father was an alcoholic who first breezed into my life when I was nine. Prince-Charming-like, he promised me the world, and then disappeared a few weeks later, giving me my first broken heart.

I've been married three times and divorced twice, but I raised my two children to be happy, successful adults and I'm now a proud grandmother of four. After my first divorce, I studied hard and became a personal skills and employment trainer and NVQ assessor – a job I did for nearly twenty years.

I was seriously injured in a major car accident in 2003. Spending many months at home recovering gave me the time to look back at the journey I had made and reassess what my priorities in life should be. I wrote a bucket list, which I've been working through steadily since then, despite the physical pain I still endure every waking moment of every day (thank God for strong painkillers). I have, to date, completed 103 items on this list, but I still have many things left to achieve…

Around that time, I also decided to pursue my writing dreams and over the last few years, I have written two sci-fi romance novels and the first book of a fantasy fiction trilogy for children (Book 2 is almost complete) – while also working part-time in administration or customer service jobs to pay the bills.

My little boat has been rocked by many waves, both high and low. In the past, I endured being bullied at work, and I suffered from depression, anxiety, and panic attacks. At times, I had to survive on government benefits, but I always clawed my way back to being financially independent. The car accident almost capsized me.

My voyage has been tumultuous: I've had many moments of pain and grief. Ones that stand out most keenly include my beloved grandparents dying, the sudden death of my brother, and watching my mother succumb to vascular dementia. Among those, I have also had moments of heady, passionate love and pure joy, the delight of watching my children grow, and the pleasure of welcoming grandchildren to the world.

Every wave has taught me that life goes on, and that like the weather out at sea, conditions change, storms blow over, and situations do improve (although they sometimes get worse first!).

I've found that keeping a wicked sense of humour has always helped me to cope with the bad times.

As a teenager, during a Religious Education class, I remember a teacher asking, 'Why does God allow so many awful things to happen to people?' Some of my classmates suggested that He was punishing people for their sins, but I knew, even then, that some of us were given trials in life for a different reason. I simply knew that eventually, when I had survived the storms, I would be stronger and wiser, and that I could become an example for others.

I'm no longer particularly religious, but I truly believe that this is the right time for me to be a lighthouse for anyone struggling in the dark, or at least a guide to help others in navigating their way ahead.

Note from Sharon

Now in my fifties, my life's journey has not been plain sailing. At times, the water was smooth. At others, there were a few ripples – but I've also faced my share of storms and tempests.

I was raised by a loving mom and dad, in a two-up two-down terraced house with my younger brother Robert and the family dog, Blackie.

My dad came from a large family and he was the one they all went to when they were in trouble or needed a safe haven. He never turned anyone away. Dad worked hard and Mom was a busy housewife. I would often spend time at my nan's as it was my safe haven in more ways than one. There, I could be ME! I played shop in my nan's kitchen, we dressed up, and I would go with her to visit her sisters. Being with my nan was definitely my happy place.

I worked hard at school, where nothing came easy to me even though I was willing and eager to learn. Throughout my school life, I had to deal with what was to be my lifelong challenge: my size and weight. I was tall for my age, with a mature attitude, but at 11 years old, I was a size 18. I was bullied and made fun of and it was always assumed that the big fat girl was stupid and there for the entertainment of others.

Sadly, this continued well into my adult life, and today, my weight is still an ongoing battle. I was diagnosed with Type 2 Diabetes. I worked hard to lose weight and keep it off, but I still have a way to go.

When I met Les, I found someone who liked me for who I was and, after a choppy start, we had a big family wedding. Like my life, my marriage was not plain sailing. We faced our share of storms along the way, but as time went by, the storms grew fewer, and we were able to enjoy the calm waters with just the occasional ripple and rumble of thunder.

In my working life, I spent most of my time in training and development, which is where I met Viv. I specialised in Apprenticeships, and I loved my job, taking great satisfaction in helping young people develop both professionally and personally so they could achieve their goals. I had a fulfilling career and worked my way up to developing and running apprenticeships for a local council, and Les supported me every step of the way.

Like Viv, a nasty accident changed all that. Due to ongoing medical issues and the need for further surgery, I lost my job. Although this was devastating, it allowed me to spend quality time with my dad, who had developed dementia, and to help my mom look after him. My dad was my hero and being there for him when he needed me the most, is something I will be forever thankful for.

This was a difficult time, but worse was to come. Les died unexpectedly, and for the first time in my life, I was alone in my own boat. Sadly, ten days later, my dad died too, and to say that my family and I were lost at sea is an understatement. How I managed to stay afloat is a story for another day.

I have been rowing my own boat for five years now, and I have been using my life experiences to help others in my role as a funeral arranger, supporting people who had lost their loved ones.

Although I valued the work I did, I knew I still had a lot to give and so much more to achieve, so working on this book with Viv has allowed me to expand my horizons.

Viv and I are not claiming to be experts and our lives have definitely not been perfect, but we hope that the knowledge we have gained from our experiences will enable us to help others to find their way to a happier life.

In writing this book and working on our supporting projects, we are both starting to row our own boats on a journey to improve the quality of our lives. If we can help others along the way, it'll be the icing on the cake.

Sam and Jo – Their Journeys

To help and support you on your journey, we would like to introduce you to Sam and Jo, our fictional rowers. At the end of each chapter, you will be able to follow their progress, their highs and their lows, and judge for yourself if they've made the right choices.

We hope that by following their stories and comparing them to your own voyage, that you will be inspired and encouraged to reflect on where you are in your life.

Sharon and Viv – Our Journey

In order to write this book (and develop our website, etc.) we had to follow our own advice, get into our boat, and start rowing. As we want to share this with you, at the end of each chapter, you will be able to follow our course and maybe even compare this to your progress as you begin to Row Your Own Boat.

There have been times when we have had to rethink our course. We've been through highs and lows, and we've had plenty of storms to face, but we have learnt a lot along the way.

We hope that sharing our experience will help and encourage you to achieve your dream of Rowing Your Own Boat.

We both sincerely hope that even if you only take on board one of our ideas, perhaps only change one little thing in your life, it helps you to improve your boat and navigate your journey. Just that will make it worth the work we've put into writing it.

We hope you enjoy the ride!

Chapter 1 – Assess Your Boat

Row, row, row your boat,

In your bubble bath,

If you can see that you've been wrong,

You are allowed to laugh.

In this chapter we cover:

- How to assess your current life position
- How to assess your achievements, skills, and personal qualities

So, as you'll have guessed, we're now going to get you to think about your life as being in a little boat (or a big one). Where you go from here is entirely up to you.

Remember, you picked up this book because you felt that you needed to do something about your life. However, before you can start to improve your boat, plot a course, and set sail on a new voyage, you need to examine exactly where you are now, and precisely why you feel a bit lost or all at sea.

The Temple of Apollo in Delphi was built in the 7th Century BC
and was where people went to consult the oracle for advice.
It is famous for the words 'Know Thyself', which
were written in the forecourt for every visitor to see.
This is still good advice today as, unless you know yourself,
you cannot appreciate where you are,
let alone decide on your future direction.

If you are ***really*** unhappy with your current boat, your recent journeys, and your voyage through life so far, and you're doubting that you'll ever achieve your dreams, you need to drop anchor and evaluate where you are right now.

Remember, this book's for you. It's yours to help with your journey. It's yours to scribble in, make notes in, lay down your innermost feelings and thoughts in. For anyone who would prefer to write elsewhere, we have a resource pack of worksheets available for you to print, simply email us at info@rowyourownboat.co.uk to request a copy.

Using this book, you can work out what to do in the future. This doesn't mean planning the rest of your life, but simply considering what you can do in the next few weeks or months, or however long it may take to reach your destination.

So, let's dive straight in.

Answer the following questions as honestly as you can (no one else need ever see this). Make as many notes as you need to – remember, this is your first assessment of the condition of your boat and your current position on the ocean of your life, so go for it!

Here are just a few of the areas you may want to look at and consider in relation to the questions:

- Relationships
- Health and fitness
- Habits
- Accommodation
- Your job
- Your leisure time (or lack of it)
- Your current financial situation

<u>Where is your boat right now?</u>

What do you like or dislike about your life and the way you're living it?

What's working well?

Could it be even better?

What's **not** working well (anything you beat yourself up over) and how would you like it to change?

On a scale of 1-10, how would you rate the general quality of your life?

What do you want to improve?

Make a list of anything in your life you'd like to change, no matter how big or small.

1.

2.

3.

4.

5.

6.

7.

8.

9.

10.

Is your life moving forwards or backwards, or are you stuck in one place?

What makes you think that?

What (or who) are you holding on to that you need to let go of?

Why?

Now look at your list and prioritise the areas you'd like to change:

1.

2.

3.

4.

5.

6.

7.

8.

9.

10.

Do you feel stuck in the doldrums?

There may be only one or two small things you'd like to change, or you might want to completely alter your whole direction and set off on a brand-new adventure.

The choice is yours, but before you can move forwards, you need to have a look back at what has brought you to this point.

<u>Evaluate where you are right now</u>

Spend a few minutes thinking about your life and make notes on how you feel (both positive and negative thoughts) about the following items, adding any personal extras you may think of:

Your physical condition

- Location/Accommodation
- Health and fitness
- Addictions

The people around you

- Family
- Friends
- Colleagues
- Customers
- Others

Your achievements and skills

- School/College/University
- Business/Career
- Hobbies/interests
- Money/finances

Now answer the following questions about your mental well-being:

- Do you often feel scared?
- Have you followed your heart or your head? Too much or not enough?
- Do you feel weak at times?
- How's your recreation and lifestyle?
- What about your personal and spiritual development?

Do you think about the things you've achieved in your life? Or do you tend to focus on the things you regret?

Many of us are not comfortable discussing our past successes, not wanting to be seen as bragging.

That means we often don't acknowledge our skills and achievements, even to ourselves.

Some of us downplay the challenges we've had to overcome to get to where we are today, while others don't recognise them at all. While completing this exercise, make sure you consider the good things you have done, as well as any negatives.

What have you achieved which will prepare you for rowing your own boat?

Let's pause to recognise and celebrate you.

We are going to use the following section to think about your achievements, your skills, and your personal qualities. You may find there is some overlap between the three sections; that doesn't matter.

These exercises are about understanding what you are good at and how well equipped your boat already is. Later, it will help you identify areas that need improvement.

Anything you've been pleased with, whatever you feel you did well, no matter how big or how small, should be included.

Some things might seem inconsequential to you, but things that are easy to some are major challenges to others, so even simple achievements, skills, and personal qualities should be counted.

<u>What Are Your Achievements?</u>

Achievements are things that you specifically have done. You may have had help, but anything that you had to put your time and effort into can count as an achievement.

Remember, achievements aren't measured by what others have achieved; they are measured by your effort, and the sense of satisfaction you derive from them.

Try to fill the following boxes with achievements you have made over the years, and don't worry if there are blanks (you can use those to guide your journey if they are areas you would like to fill in!).

Physical	Add your notes here:
Exercised regularly	
Lost weight	
Overcame an addiction	
Started a hobby or activity	
Built something	
Decorated a room or house	
Lived by yourself	
Mental	
Dealt with a big change in your life	
Got through a bad time	
Overcame a fear	
Solved a problem	
Learnt from your mistakes	

People	
Cared for family	
Helped friends	
Supported colleagues	
Served customers	
Befriended strangers	
Sorted out an argument/conflict	
Joined a group	
Taught something to someone	
Worked in a team	
Led or managed people	
Talked to a big group	
Raised money for charity	

Now add your own items:

Your Skills

Simply put, a skill is the ability to do something – for example, the ability to manage a budget, use a computer, or drive a car.

You probably know there are some things you're not absolutely brilliant at, but you already have many skills which you can use, or add to, to improve your boat and prepare for your journey.

Thinking about and identifying the skills you already have may give you new ideas for what you want or need to do in the future. It will highlight the opportunities you can grasp right now with your existing skills as a starting point. It will also highlight what you may need to change in order to start rowing your own boat and set off towards a new, better life.

You might not recognise some of the routine things you do as skills, but other people would, so if you can't think of anything, ask your family or friends what they think you're good at.

Now, grab a piece of paper and a pen, or open a blank file on your computer, and think back over your life – your health, home life, friends, education, training, career, and hobbies.

Start to make a list of everything that you **can** do.

Once you have your list, take a look at the following suggestions and highlight the things you enjoy or those which bring you the most satisfaction.

Can you?

- Drive
- Manage your time well
- Organise things
- Absorb and remember facts
- Learn new things
- Study for and pass exams or tests easily
- Read and take on new information
- Follow instructions or understand diagrams and blueprints
- Install and/or operate new equipment (TV/Computer, etc.)
- Operate machinery
- Plan ahead
- Speak another language

Have you ever?

- Changed the way you work
- Repaired things
- Received an award for doing something
- Got a job or promotion, or been given an extra responsibility
- Thought up or shared a new idea
- Managed a budget or cut costs
- Written for a newsletter, etc.

Are you creative – can you?

- Design things
- Take good photographs
- Care for living things (people/animals/plants)
- Cook
- Draw or paint
- Decorate

Now take another look at your list and check you haven't missed anything out that will help you to *Row Your Own Boat*.

Knowing who you are and identifying your strengths and weaknesses is the best starting point for any personal journey.

What are your personal qualities?

What kind of person do you think you are? What qualities do you have?

In this section, you should look at how well you get on with other people, how you behave in different circumstances, etc. Your personal qualities are the attitudes/habits you've developed over time. They are the things that make you different from everyone else.

In the lists below, circle any that apply to you now (don't be afraid to tick the 'both' box if your qualities are different in different situations).

Positive Qualities	Both	Negative Qualities
Calm		Worried
Friendly		Unsociable
Nice		Unpleasant
Reliable		Unreliable
Honest		Dishonest
Flexible		Inflexible
Organised		Chaotic
Assertive		Aggressive
Decisive		Indecisive
Creative		Unoriginal
Competitive		Unenthusiastic
Co-operative		Unhelpful

Self-disciplined		Out of control
Self-sufficient		Reliant on others
Brave		Cautious
Self-confident		Shy
Keen to learn		Disinterested
Sensitive		Uncaring
Stylish		Unkempt
Industrious		Idle
Down-to-earth		Idealistic
Inventive		Unenterprising
Responsible		Reckless

Now examine the list and decide which qualities have helped you to get on in life and which have held you back.

Are there any qualities you'd like to change? If so, highlight them.

Now we come to the final part – let's have a good look at your boat.

Once again, add anything you want to work on to your list or highlight it; these are important notes you'll be looking back at later.

Physical

Am I healthy?

How's my diet and weight?

Do I get enough exercise?

Have I got enough stamina?

Emotional/mental

How am I feeling – happy and content or sad and depressed?

Am I happy and at peace when alone, or do I get lonely?

Do I follow my heart, my head, or my intuition?

Do I like myself or do I criticise or feel ashamed of myself?

Do I need to forgive myself for anything?

Do I have emotional baggage or a secret I am worried about others discovering?

What or who makes me sad, fearful, or angry?

Can I control my emotions?

Do I overreact?

What do I feel most passionate about?

Am I selfish, childish, or irresponsible in any way?

Am I suffering from stress? What's causing it? How do I handle it?

Do I feel a need to keep busy?

Do I have a lot of negative thoughts?

What lies do I tell myself?

What problems and life crises have I been through? Have any of these been repeated?

Do I blame others and moan about the things they have that I don't have?

Do I feel frustrated, flat, or stuck?

Do I bottle things up?

If I could start over, who or how would I like to be?

People/relationships

Who do I spend most of my time with? Friends? Relatives? Colleagues?

Is the time I spend with them quality time or not?

Are they negative or positive people?

Do they support and encourage or drain me?

Do I depend on them for something?

Do their agendas interfere with my life?

Do I need better, more satisfying relationships?

Am I too competitive, or not competitive enough?

Do I judge people harshly?

Do I play mind games with others or are they playing games with me?

What do people say about me and do these opinions concern me?

Successes/failures

What do I feel I have succeeded at?

What failures have I had?

What am I proud of?

Do I fear success and self-sabotage myself with limiting beliefs?

What do I want to achieve in the remainder of my life?

Employment

What gives me the motivation to succeed?

Am I earning enough?

Does the money I earn work well for me?

Is my work-life balance good?

Is job satisfaction more important than financial rewards?

Is any part of my life NOT what I would choose?

Identifying any changes you want to make
to have the best life you can have
will take you a step closer to living it.

After everything you've looked at in this chapter, answer the following questions honestly:

Where am I now?

Is any part of my life <u>not</u> what I would choose?

What do I want (or need) to change?

You now know what your boat is currently like, and how well equipped you are for a journey. The first task of assessing your boat (and situation) is complete!

Sam was born and raised in the UK and has worked in hospitality since leaving school, starting as a Trainee Hotel Receptionist. He gained his first receptionist job with a large hotel chain and after a few years, he was promoted to Senior Receptionist. Sam went on every training course offered to staff and eventually worked his way up the ladder to Reception Manager.

Sam worked long hours, on rotating antisocial shifts, but he enjoyed his job and the challenges it brought, despite becoming aware that his current position was as far as the company would let his role develop.

However, Sam realised that he wanted more from life – more sociable hours, more time to pursue new hobbies and new relationships, or even to become independent by starting a small business.

Sam just wanted more!

When another attempt at starting a relationship failed because he didn't have enough time to devote to it over the Christmas and New Year period, Sam knew it was time for a change. He decided to take a long hard look at where he was and where he wanted to be. For the last fifteen years, his work had been his life, to the detriment of everything else. That had to change.

Not long after the breakup, Sam overheard a conversation between two of the hotel's guests about how well the launch of their business had gone. They were bubbling with enthusiasm, pride, and happiness – things Sam hadn't felt for a long time.

Sam began to think about what he needed to do to kick-start the next stage of his life, plan new goals, and decide how he could get to where he wanted to be. If he wasn't going to spend another fifteen years – or more – behind a hotel desk, he needed to act.

Unsure of the route he wanted to follow, Sam spent a few days examining every aspect of his life and wrote a list of things he wanted to change – which turned out to be basically everything.

First, he assessed his physical health. He appreciated that despite being a little overweight, enjoying the occasional drink, and not having the best diet (mainly due to his long hours and rotating shift patterns), he had no real health problems. However, he did want to improve his fitness.

Next, he weighed up his achievements and skills. Even though he did not yet know exactly what he wanted to do to change his life, Sam knew that a lot of his skills could transfer to various other roles. At the hotel, he had an excellent rapport with his staff and customers, he had good management and organisational skills, and he was quick to learn new methods of working.

He decided to jot down everything he could think of and make lists he could refer to later.

Sam's answers to some of the questions in Chapter 1 would have looked something like this:

Q: Where is MY boat right now?
A: Adrift, no direction, no destination in sight.

Q: What do you like or dislike about your life and the way you are living it?
A: Antisocial hours. All work and no play. No prospect of promotion.

Q: What is working well?
A: Good at my job.

Q: What could be made even better?
A: Salary, relationships, health and fitness.

Q: What is not working well?
A: No promotion prospects and poor work-life balance.

Q: On a scale of 1-10, how would you rate the general quality of your life?
A: 5

What I want to improve:

1. ***Work-life balance***
2. ***Relationships – family and friends***
3. ***Partner (lack of)***
4. ***Health and fitness***

Q: Is my life going forwards or backwards, or stuck?
A: STUCK.

Q: What makes you think that?
A: Nothing will change if I stay in my current job.

Q: What (or who) are you holding on to that you need to let go of?
A: Job security? Old habits?

Physical Condition

Location/Accommodation: ***OK.***

Health and fitness: ***Need to lose some weight and get fitter.***

People ***I get on well with everyone but can't see family & friends as much as I'd like to.***
I want to find someone special.

Achievements and Skills

Business/career ***Doing well in my role but can't get any higher up the ladder.***

Hobbies/interests ***Nothing outside of work lately & old hobbies dropped due to working life.***

Money/finances ***Not earning a fortune but OK – would like more eventually.***

Mental well-being

Followed my head too much: ***Yes – lifestyle doesn't work now.***

What are your achievements?

Physical	Add your notes here:
Exercised regularly	***Used to but not lately.***
Lost weight	
Overcame an addiction	
Started a hobby or activity	
Built something	
Decorated a room or house	***Yes, my whole house when I first moved in.***
Lived by yourself	***Yes.***

Mental	
Dealt with a big change in your life	***When my dad died.***
Got through a bad time	***When my dad died.***
Overcame a fear	
Solved a problem	***Every day at work!***
Learnt from your mistakes	***Like to think so.***
People	
Cared for family	***Not enough, Mum needs more help than I can give due to work.***
Helped friends	***Not as much as I used to.***
Supported colleagues	***Constantly.***
Served customers	***Every day.***
Befriended strangers	***Occasionally.***
Sorted out an argument/conflict	***Between staff and/or customers.***
Joined a group	
Taught something to someone	***Trained new staff.***
Worked in a team	***Every day.***
Led or managed people	***Every day.***
Talked to a big group	***Often lead team meetings.***
Raised money for charity	
Now add your own items:	

Skills

I can:

Drive.

Manage my time well.

Organise things and plan ahead.

Learn new things and pass exams or tests easily.

Absorb and remember facts.

Read and take on new information.

Follow instructions or understand diagrams and blueprints.

Install and/or operate new equipment (TV/Computer, etc.)

In the past I have:

Changed the way the team and I work.

Repaired things.

Got a job, promotions, and been given extra responsibility.

Thought up or shared new ideas.

Managed a budget and cut costs at work.

My creative side – I can:

Cook.

Decorate.

Positive Qualities	Both	Negative Qualities
Calm	✓	Worried
Friendly ✓		Unsociable
Nice ✓		Unpleasant
Reliable ✓		Unreliable
Honest ✓		Dishonest
Flexible ✓		Inflexible
Organised ✓		Chaotic
Assertive ✓		Aggressive
Decisive ✓		Indecisive
Creative	✓	Unoriginal
Competitive	✓	Unenthusiastic

Co-operative ✓		Unhelpful
Self-disciplined ✓		Out of control
Self-sufficient ✓		Reliant on others
Brave	✓	Cautious
Self-confident	✓	Shy
Keen to learn	✓	Disinterested
Sensitive ✓		Uncaring
Stylish ✓		Unkempt
Industrious ✓		Idle
Down-to-earth	✓	Idealistic
Inventive	✓	Unenterprising
Responsible ✓		Reckless

PHYSICAL

Am I healthy? ***Not really.***

How's my diet and weight? ***Needs work.***

Do I get enough exercise? ***No.***

Have I got enough stamina? ***Yes.***

EMOTIONAL/MENTAL

How am I feeling? Am I happy and content, or sad and depressed?

Somewhere in between.

Am I happy and at peace when alone, or do I get lonely? ***Feel lonelier now I'm older!***

Do I follow my heart, my head, or my intuition? ***Depends – but mainly head.***

Do I like myself or do I criticise or feel ashamed of myself? ***I think I'm OK.***

Do I need to forgive myself for anything? ***No.***

Do I have emotional baggage or a secret I am worried about others discovering? ***No.***

What or who makes me sad, fearful, or angry? ***Being alone and worried that I'll never have a good relationship or a family of my own makes me sad. Being stuck in a job with no further prospects makes me fearful – can't do this for the next thirty years.***

What do I feel most passionate about? **Forgot what that feels like – it used to be work, but not anymore.**

Am I selfish, childish, or irresponsible in any way? **Don't think so...**

Am I suffering from stress and do I know what is causing it? **Not sure.**

How do I handle stress? **I try to ignore it.**

Do I feel a need to keep busy? **Only at work.**

Do I find myself thinking a lot of negative thoughts? **No.**

What lies do I tell myself? **That I'm happy as things are.**

What problems and life crises have I been through? **Dad died.**

Have any of these been repeated? **No.**

Do I moan about the things others have, and I don't have? **No.**

Where do I feel frustrated, flat, or stuck? **At work – need to be more fulfilled!**

If I could start over, who or how would I like to be? **Working for myself with regular hours.**

PEOPLE/RELATIONSHIPS

Who do I spend most of my time with? Friends? Relatives? Colleagues? **Colleagues.**

Is the time I spend with them quality time or not? **No – it's all work-related.**

Are they negative or positive people? **Many are negative.**

Do they support and encourage or drain me? **Drain.**

Do I depend on them for something? **To help me to maintain the hotel's standards.**

Do their agendas interfere with my life? **Sometimes.**

Do I need better, more satisfying relationships? **YES!**

Am I too competitive, or not competitive enough? **Not enough.**

Do I judge people harshly? **No (I don't think so).**

Do I play emotional/mind games with others or are they playing games with me? **Not that I'm aware of.**

What do people say about me? ***Friends say that I'm all work and no play.***

Does their opinion of me bother me at all? ***Yes – feel guilty at times for not seeing them.***

SUCCESSES/FAILURES

What do I feel I have succeeded at? ***My job.***

What failures have I had? ***Relationships.***

What am I proud of? ***My Job – but it's not enough.***

Do I fear success and self-sabotage myself with limiting beliefs? ***Maybe.***

What do I want to achieve in the remainder of my life? ***Successful in business, good relationships, and be fitter and healthier.***

EMPLOYMENT

What gives me the motivation to succeed? ***Recognition, job satisfaction.***

Am I earning enough? ***No.***

Does the money I do have work for me? ***Just.***

Is my work-life balance good? ***No.***

Is job satisfaction more important than financial rewards? ***Yes.***

What do I want to change?

- ***Need to lose weight and get fitter so I'll have more energy and look better.***
- ***I need to be more fulfilled (by running my own business???)***
- ***Would like to see more of my friends and family.***
- ***Would like to have a special relationship with someone.***

As Sam examined his life, took stock of what was most important to him, and began to think about building a more positive future, COVID-19 began to affect the UK.

Jo, a wife and mother, had two children. Jack was in his final year in sixth form and Cassie was away at university. Her husband James had his own architect's firm, where Jo worked part-time as an administrator.

Jo was close to her parents, who were both in their late 70s, and often called in to see them on her way home from work. She shopped for them regularly, and often cooked for them as well.

On the last Friday of every month, Jo usually met a small group of friends for lunch. A mix of males and females, they had all been in school together and had remained good friends ever since.

At their February gathering, Jo found herself sitting next to Sam, who was much quieter than usual. When they had finished eating, Jo gave him a nudge.

'Sam, you've been really quiet today. Are you OK?'

He nodded. 'Sort of.'

'What does that mean?'

'I'm at a crossroads, I think.' He gave her a weak smile. 'I've been thinking about my life and, well... I suppose I've realised that I'm not as happy as I thought I was.'

Jo blinked. 'Why? Has something happened?'

He shook his head. 'No, although I'm a bit concerned about this virus thing getting out of hand. It's not that, though… I'm just not happy with anything right now. I'm nearly forty-five and I want to do something different. I need more free time and less antisocial hours.' He glanced at their other lunch companions. 'I want the kind of life most of you guys have.'

'Trust me.' Jo scoffed. 'You wouldn't want my life!'

He raised his eyebrows. 'Why not? I mean, you've got James and the kids, a job you love, and parents who adore you. What's wrong with that?'

'It's not what you think.' She paused and considered for a moment. 'It's not that it's bad, it's just… well, I don't think anyone is ***really*** *happy, are they? Don't you think we all just fall into our slot in the world? We float along with the people around us and do what's expected of us.'*

Sam frowned. 'Is that how you feel?'

She nodded. 'Most of the time. Don't get me wrong, it's not a problem. I suppose I've kind of got used to it. We all just have to get on with our lives, don't we?'

'Why?'

She gave him a blank look.

'Jo, I want more than I've been getting out of life.' Sam shrugged. 'I want to make a change. I want to follow through with some of the ideas I've had over the years but never been brave enough to do.' He smiled at her. 'I'm going to make a new start, I think.'

'How?'

Sam looked a little embarrassed, shrugging again. 'Well… I've been making lists, looking at everything in my life, all the good bits and especially the things I know I need to change, and I'm going to plot a new course to take.'

'Can I help?' she offered. 'I'd be interested in seeing what you're doing.'

Sam raised an eyebrow. 'Haven't you got enough to do? You're always rushed off your feet.'

Jo shrugged. 'I have a couple of spare hours here and there. I want to help. Really.'

'I'll think about it.' Sam smiled at her, so she nodded and decided to let it go for now.

Unlike Sam and Jo, we began our journey in June 2020, on the first day we could meet after the first UK COVID-19 lockdown.

Having spent many years working in the training and development industry, which we both loved and valued, life had taken us in different directions. We'd had our share of storms along the way, but in 2020, we both found ourselves at a stage in our lives where we felt we had more to give. Writing *Row Your Own Boat* would be a good start.

In our day jobs, we were both in key worker roles, (Viv as a merchandiser in many supermarkets and Sharon as a funeral arranger), providing much-needed services as the world faced the COVID-19 pandemic, but we both felt we could be happier.

In our first *Row Your Own Boat* discussions, we looked at where we were and where we wanted to be. Here is the list of things we wanted to do:

1. *Use our skills and expertise to help others by supporting them as they examine and improve their lives.*
2. *Help people feel happier and encourage them to pursue their goals.*
3. *Inspire others to learn new skills and to take on new challenges.*
4. *Share our experiences and the lessons we have learnt along the way to help others.*
5. *Take the opportunity to work together again on a project that is important to us.*
6. *Set up our own business, working for ourselves.*
7. *Challenge ourselves to learn new skills and update existing ones.*
8. *Take charge of our own destinies, get into our boats, and start rowing.*
9. *Feel happier and live our best lives.*
10. *Row Our Own Boats (but together, at least for this project).*

We were getting older, we'd both had our share of health problems to deal with, and neither of us knew what the future might hold.

The one thing we had both taken from our journey through life, together with the pandemic, was that you should not put off till tomorrow what you can do today.

If we were going to pursue our dream, the time was now!

To write this book, we began by looking at the skills we had between us which would help us to reach our destination.

We can:

- *Drive (and have our own cars)*
- *Manage our time well, working to deadlines*
- *Plan ahead*
- *Organise information, schedules, people, and events*
- *Learn new skills*
- *Read and take on new information*
- *Change and adapt our working methods*
- *Take on new responsibilities*
- *Develop and share ideas and processes*
- *Manage a budget*
- *Effectively communicate in every way*
- *Research and share information*
- *Balance the needs of the company against the needs of our customers*

We also looked at our combined personal qualities, which would help us on our way to reaching our destination.

Positive Qualities	Both	Negative Qualities
Calm		Worried ✓
Friendly ✓		Unsociable
Nice ✓		Unpleasant
Reliable ✓		Unreliable
Honest ✓		Dishonest
Flexible ✓		Inflexible
Organised	✓	Chaotic
Assertive	✓	Aggressive
Decisive ✓		Indecisive
Creative ✓		Unoriginal
Competitive ✓		Unenthusiastic
Co-operative ✓		Unhelpful
Self-disciplined	✓	Out of control
Self-sufficient	✓	Reliant on others
Brave		Cautious ✓
Self-confident	✓	Shy
Keen to learn ✓		Disinterested
Sensitive ✓		Uncaring
Stylish ✓		Unkempt
Industrious ✓		Idle
Down-to-earth	✓	Idealistic
Inventive	✓	Unenterprising
Responsible	✓	Reckless

We then looked at our boats to see if they were up to the task ahead. We had to be honest with each other. At the end of the first lockdown, when we were keen to start this project, we were both tired and stressed from having worked daily in our key roles. However, despite being in rocky waters, our boats were in good shape, and we felt confident in our abilities.

Below are some of our answers to the questions we asked in this section:

PHYSICAL

Are we healthy? ***Not as healthy as we could be.***

How's our diet and weight? ***Could be better.***

Do we get enough exercise? ***Again, could do more.***

Have we got enough stamina? ***Yes.***

EMOTIONAL/MENTAL

How are we feeling? ***Feeling OK, but could be happier, naturally concerned with what the future will hold.***

Are we happy and at peace when alone, or do we get lonely? ***Yes to both.***

Do we follow our hearts, our heads, or our intuition? ***At times, all of them.***

What or who makes us sad, fearful, or angry? ***People who are not following the government's guidelines to help us fight the pandemic, putting us all at risk.***

What do we feel most passionate about? ***Caring for those we love, trying to keep them safe during the pandemic.***

Are we selfish, childish, or irresponsible in any way? ***Generally, no, although at times we can all be a little selfish and maybe even childish!***

Do we feel a need to keep busy? ***Yes, but as key workers, we are both busy.***

What problems and life crises have we been through? Have any of these been repeated? ***We have both had our share of health problems, we have both suffered the loss of loved ones and yes, we have both experienced these more than once.***

If we could start over, who or how would we like to be?
Sharon – In hindsight, I should have resat my Statistics A-Level to continue with my application to become an Executive Officer in the Civil Service. I had already passed the entrance exam, one of only four who

had passed out of the 150 who sat the exam. Instead, I accepted a permanent job at Birmingham Airport, where I had been working during the summer.

Viv – Looking back, I wish I had been able to take the next level of my digital photography qualifications. Unfortunately, funding was not available in my area, and I could not afford to pay for it at the time. My dream of going into business as a photographer was shelved.

PEOPLE/RELATIONSHIPS

Who do we spend most of our time with? Friends? Relatives? Colleagues? Is the time we spend with them quality time or not? ***COVID-19 has made spending time with people other than our colleagues and those we live with (or are in a support bubble with) difficult, especially as we are both very sociable people. We both value the quality time we can spend with others more than we did before.***

SUCCESSES/FAILURES

What do we feel that we have succeeded at? ***Facing our share of storms and coming through them stronger and more determined to live our best lives.***

What do we want to achieve in the remainder of our life? ***To row our own boats while encouraging and supporting others in doing the same.***

EMPLOYMENT

Is our work-life balance good? ***Currently NO, as our roles as key workers have made us busier than ever.***

Is job satisfaction more important than financial rewards? ***Definitely YES!***

WHERE ARE WE NOW?

Ready to get into our boats and start rowing.

WHAT DO WE WANT/NEED TO CHANGE?

We both need a feeling of achievement in our lives. Writing this book will be a good start.

Chapter 2 – Identify Your Destination

Row, row, row your boat,

Plan the way to go,

It could be here, it could be there,

Only you will know.

In this chapter we cover:

- How to choose a destination
- What obstacles need to be addressed first

So you've had a good look at where you are now, how you got here, and all the good and maybe not so good things about your boat and the journey you've been on to date.

At the end of the previous chapter, you should have been able to answer the question:

What do I WANT or NEED to change?

Now it's time to look at your answers and chart the route you want to take to move forward.

> *"The secret of change is to focus all of your energy not on fighting the old, but on building the new."*
>
> *Socrates*

So **RIGHT NOW**, at this moment, what do you think would give you the most satisfaction in your life?

Is there something you'd like to accomplish?

Getting a new job?

Making more money?

Starting a new hobby?

Improving your relationships?

Improving your health?

Taking on a new challenge?

Can you identify a life purpose that you think you should be addressing?

What things give you the most pleasure? Your family? Career? Hobbies?

Would a meaningful life be one where you could spend most of your time on these things?

Is there a legacy you'd like to leave for others, or knowledge you'd like to pass on?

In your ideal dream world, if you had all the time and money you needed, if you had fewer family or work responsibilities, and if you knew that you could not possibly fail, what would you really want to do with the rest of your life?

What would your perfect day be like?

Now is the time to listen to your heart and use your knowledge and experience to plan your journey.

If you don't chart a course and follow it, your boat will either be forever stuck in the doldrums or simply bobbing around, buffeted by the storms and waves, thrust in all directions, and you'll never get to your destination.

Find a quiet spot, somewhere you can sit and mull over your life for a while. Think about everything you feel is important to you, and begin to define your personal goals for everything – your relationships, health, employment, financial situation, accommodation, etc.

Start by answering these questions (you can make notes in the table on the next page):

- What would my definition of success be?
- What would I like to accomplish?
- What could I do to make my life better, to feel satisfied?
- What can I do to make myself feel proud?
- Do I have any special gifts I want to share with others?

- At the end of my life, what is the one regret I absolutely do not want to have?
- What is my life's dream or vision?
- Out of all my dreams, hopes, and wishes, which ones are the most important to me?
- Which ones would give me the satisfaction I crave?

MY DREAMS, HOPES, AND WISHES:	
1	
2	
3	
4	
5	
6	
7	
8	
9	
10	

Look at your list. In the past, have you ever started to work towards any of these things but put them off?

If so, why?

Have you ever said to yourself, 'The time's not right to do it now; I'll do it "*whenever*"?'

Yes?

What is your '*whenever*'?

Does your '*whenever*' include things like:

- When I feel better or less stressed
- When the kids start school
- When the kids leave school
- When the house has been decorated
- When I've found the right course
- When I get a new job
- When I can afford it
- When I retire

So (and now you need to be completely honest with yourself), what is **really** holding you back?

Negative thoughts can often stop us from doing things. If you worry about what other people think of you, you'll never do anything. If you decide you are too old or too stupid to achieve something, then you will be.

Maybe it's time to look at your attitudes and shift your mindset?

To begin this process, you could start by researching information about:

- Ways you can improve yourself physically and mentally
- Educational courses
- Employment opportunities
- People who may have been in the same position as you, but who now live fabulous, passionate lives. If they did it, you can too.

You can steer your boat towards
any destination you choose!

Yes, there may be genuine reasons why you can't implement a massive life change right now, but you can start to plan – *really plan* – and plot the direction you want to steer your boat in as soon as you're able to.

Before COVID-19, none of us dreamed we would be in lockdown for weeks on end. Some people used that time to learn new skills or to reassess their attitudes to life. Others simply got through to the best of their abilities. Many people had their lives put on hold, but their dreams remained intact.

If COVID-19 has taught us anything, it's that unexpected things happen and the only true constant in life is that everything changes.

Things we never dreamed of may knock the oars out of our hands, but we all have the same options: we can float where we are, or we can pick the oars back up and hope, plan, and work towards a better life journey.

Where would you like to be in six months? How about a year from now? Five years? Ten?

Do you want to be exactly where you are now, or would you rather be somewhere different?

What would give your life purpose or meaning?

What do you do that makes you happy, and do you do it enough?

Do you want to make a mark on the world, achieve fame and fortune, or simply leave precious memories for your family and friends?

What would you like people to say about you at your funeral?

What changes could you make to keep your current comfort and security, but be able to spend more time on meaningful things that will give you happiness?

In the past, did you dream about achieving certain goals? What happened to those dreams?

Would you still like to do any of them?

What is stopping you?

Sometimes, it's only your own thoughts (especially the ones which say that you're not worthy of anything) that are stopping you from planning and making your life's journey better.

Einstein said, '*Logic can take you from A to B, but imagination will take you everywhere.*' If you can imagine something, you can do it.

Right?

But how?

First, you need to identify what you need to change to improve your boat.

So, what needs to change?

Look back at your DREAMS, HOPES, AND WISHES list and, being as honest as you can, think about the things in your life you may need to work on to bring your dreams, hopes, and wishes closer to reality.

Read the lists on the following pages and highlight anything that rings true to you.

Don't worry about how, or when, or what you may need to do to change things at this point. You're simply going to produce a rough working list of things you want to look at in order to start your journey. You might find the examples below helpful, or you might wish to focus on entirely different things.

To work towards my dreams, hopes, and wishes, I feel that I need to work on:

My health

- Improving my fitness levels (taking up or increasing exercise)
- Addressing a medical issue and/or handling it better
- Reducing pain or recovering from a trauma
- Improving my diet (eat healthier foods) or my appearance
- Reducing my weight
- Recovering from addiction (alcohol, drugs, nicotine)
- Addressing a sexual concern

Mental well-being

- Taking responsibility for my own life
- Offloading draining responsibilities
- Handling big life events better (births, deaths, marriages, separations, or moving to new locations)
- Becoming more positive
- Seeking help to handle mental problems
- Becoming more spiritual (regularly meditating or praying)
- Developing more patience
- Enjoying life more and having fun
- Learning how to handle stress better
- Following creative talents
- Taking up a new hobby

Relationships

- Dealing with and moving on from previous bad relationship experiences
- Ending a negative or draining relationship
- Attracting new people into my life
- Finding or further developing a loving relationship
- Strengthening relations with my spouse, partner, family, and friends
- Improving communication skills
- Being more social

Career

- Designing and following a new career path
- Starting a new job or going for new opportunities
- Improving work-life balance
- Getting a raise or promotion

- Improving my education (or obtaining job training)
- Getting a coach or mentor
- Becoming more productive
- Starting a business

Financial

- Dealing with a money problem or bankruptcy
- Not overspending
- Setting up and following a budget and/or paying off debts
- Increasing my income
- Starting to save or invest
- Planning for retirement
- Buying a home

When you make your own version of this list, don't be afraid of dreaming big; no one else is going to see this unless you show it to them. Add everything you can think of which would improve your life and make you happier in the long run.

Now look over your list, but this time, ask yourself:

'***What's in it for me?***'

If you're not sure why something is on your list, reconsider it.

What do you <u>really</u> want?

If you're still not sure, don't think about the actual physical things you'd like to get, but how you think you'll feel when you get them.

What do you think achieving your goals will bring you?

Happiness? Peace? Contentment? Love? Respect?

Look at your list again and delete anything which you feel even a little unsure of (you can always add items again later if you decide they are important to your future well-being).

For everything on your list, consider why you want to do that thing or achieve that particular goal.

What will you get from it?

How will it improve your life?

If you can't define the benefits or decide why you've included an item, ***delete it***.

Now, look at your list again. If something is on it because you think it will please someone else, ***delete it***.

Having worked through these lists, you should be left with several points that you would like to work on or develop further. At this stage, you might have a clear destination in mind, or it may need more work.

If you know exactly what you want to do and where you want to be (e.g., setting up your own business, learning to drive, signing up for a new course, etc.), the next stage is to plan how you are going to reach your destination, and this is covered in the following chapter.

However, if you're still unsure about where you want to be, your course may have to include stopping points which mean that you are moving forward, but the destination is not yet fixed. Equally, some more ambitious journeys simply cannot be undertaken in one massive step and will need to be broken down into more manageable parts.

Look again at what is left on your lists and break each item down into smaller, more manageable goals. For example, if the list shows that your health could be better, this could be your first destination, because we all need our boats to be seaworthy. You don't have to launch into a tough exercise routine instantly; just start with something gentle and work up from there.

Next, look at your mental well-being. What stands out on this list? Do you need to put yourself first and learn to say 'no' to others? Would taking up a new hobby or rekindling your passion for an old interest help to address how you feel?

Choose a goal that is not too daunting and begin working towards it – and before you know it, you'll be on your way.

If you continue to work through all the sections, looking at each of the points in turn, by the end of the process, you should have all the information you need to start planning the route to your destination.

Remember:

Your goals have to be your own.

At this moment, you must be absolutely true to yourself and your innermost feelings. Yes, other people may not approve and may try to stop you (we'll deal with handling that in Chapter 5 – Your Crew), but this is your life, and no one else's.

Here's a final thought for this chapter:

Imagine yourself standing near the coast. You have a camera drone which you send high up into the sky so you can see the towns and villages nearby.

You are looking for the route to **Success Point.**

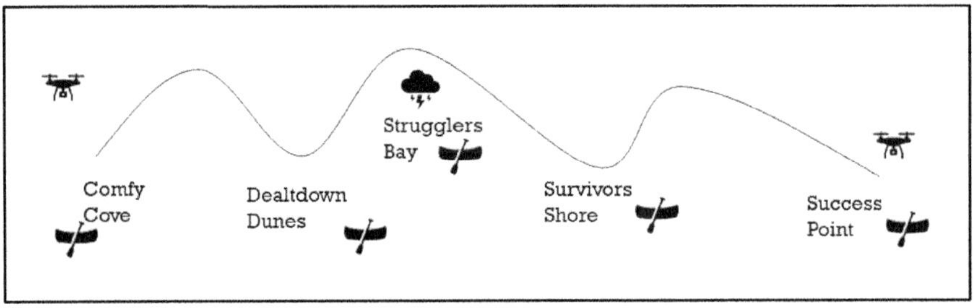

First to come into view is **<u>Comfy Cove.</u>** Here, there are masses of little boats all sheltered together. Their occupants are quite content to stay where they are; they are happy with their lives and the people around them, and they accept their place in the world. They've never questioned whether this is where they belong.

The next bay you find is flanked by **<u>Dealtdown Dunes.</u>** This is where people live who used to have dreams, but they faced a few setbacks and have now completely given up any hope of ever succeeding. They're not happy, but they're too scared to risk doing anything about it in case they fail again.

<u>Strugglers Bay</u> is a little further along. Here is where you see many people rowing their boats out on the sea. The waves are pounding them, the wind is blowing a gale, but they are determined; they know where they're heading and will struggle on.

Survivors Shore is next to come into view. Those who have got this far have defeated their problems. They've reached what they thought was their destination, but they're not as happy as they had hoped they would be. They're sitting in their boats, wondering what to do next. Should they accept where they are, or start rowing towards a new destination?

At the end of the flight, your drone spots **Success Point**. Here are all the people who have succeeded in their journeys. They've reached their goals. Some of them have travelled through many storms along the way, but they're now safe, happy, and content.

Where are you on this journey?

Now plan your own route to get to your success point.

Sam's voyage cont'd... **April 2020**

As Sam began to look more closely at his life, the Coronavirus pandemic hit the UK. The hotel was closed due to the first lockdown and Sam was furloughed.

Now Sam had the one thing he had lacked when he was working – ***TIME!***

Initially, despite the stress of the pandemic, he felt in holiday mode. He enjoyed the novelty of not working and spent the first couple of weeks catching up on movies and TV shows. He surprised family and friends by making more contact with them (via video and telephone calls), than he had done for years, so despite having to shelter at home alone, he felt more connected than he had for a long time.

At the end of April, five weeks into the lockdown, while on his weekly visit to the supermarket, Sam caught sight of his reflection in the window and was shocked. He was wearing jogging pants (as most of his trousers were feeling tight), but he had not realised how much weight he had gained by snacking on crisps and pizza and drinking a few more cans of beer and bottles of wine than usual. He did not recognise the couch potato staring back at him.

It was time to do something positive to improve his life. The lockdown was granting him the time to decide where he wanted to be and what he needed to do to get there. Pandemic or no pandemic, he could still plan for the future.

At home, Sam picked up his notes and decided it was time to take action. He read through what he had written about where he was, and then sat down to draw up a list of his dreams, hopes, and wishes.

While he was working, he mulled over the conversation he'd had with Jo a few weeks ago. Had she been right when she'd said that most people go with the flow and fall into their slot in life without realising it? Had he too easily slotted himself into working at the hotel, and could he really change that?

He could see his work there had come to a dead-end, and he wasn't inclined to branch out and look for the same work with better promotion prospects. He wanted to try something different, something that would let him manage his work-life balance and not be dictated to by others.

He also realised that there was something else he had wanted since he was a boy, and that was a dog; if he could have more regular hours or become his own boss, that could be a real possibility.

The more he thought about it, the happier he felt, and if just thinking about it made him feel that way, how would he feel if he actually broke away from his stuck-in-a rut life?

To head towards a new, self-employed career, he would have to chart his own course and start moving ahead by himself, instead of drifting along or being carried by others.

He took time to write his thoughts down:

<u>What do I WANT or NEED to change?</u>

<u>Life purpose?</u>

> ***Not sure – but running an events business would help people to enjoy big days in their lives.***
> ***Having a family would be good.***

<u>Most pleasure from?</u>

> ***Helping/serving others.***

<u>Legacy?</u>

> ***Have a family and leave kids a successful business.***

<u>MY DREAMS, HOPES AND WISHES:</u>

> ***Run my own business – be my own boss with no more awkward shift patterns.***
> ***Enjoy life – see more of family and friends.***
> ***Get a dog (and have more exercise by walking it).***
> ***Find someone special to settle down with.***

<u>What's in it for me?</u>

> ***Work freedom and independence.***
> ***Financial gains?***
> ***Happiness.***
> ***Better social life and relationships.***

<u>Where do I want to be in six months?</u>

> ***Working for myself (maybe part-time employment until the business grows?)***

In a year from now?

> ***Working full time in the business and earning enough to live on.***

Five years?

> ***Successful with regular customers/repeat business.***
> ***In a good relationship with someone special.***

Ten?

> ***Well off, independent, and maybe have kids?***

When he had finished, Sam read through all his notes. Was he being realistic? Could he really hope to implement what he was thinking about? He needed a second opinion, so he picked up the phone to call Jo. After checking in with her about life in general and how things were going, he pulled his notes towards him and steeled his nerves.

'Hey, by the way, do you remember at our last lunch when you offered to help me with my plans to change some of my life?'

'Yes, of course.'

'Have you got time to have a look at a few things I've been thinking about? I've made some notes and stuff.'

'Sure. What do you want me to do?'

'Well… just give me your opinion, really. Tell me if you think I'm being realistic or not.'

'OK, sure. Can you email them to me?'

'Yes, I'll do it now. Thanks, Jo! Also...' Sam paused, feeling awkward. 'Can you not mention it to anyone else yet? I'm just sort of… dipping my toes in, thinking about stuff…'

'Don't worry, Sam, I'll keep it confidential. Can't wait to see what you send me!'

Jo received Sam's email shortly after his call. As soon as she had a quiet moment, she settled down to read it.

> *Hi Jo,*
>
> *Thank you for looking at this for me. Please let me know what you think.*
>
> *I was quite surprised by the things you said at our last lunch as I thought you were really happy with your life, and from the look on your face at the time, I think you thought the same about me.*
>
> *I don't want to make any waves, but I've watched for years as you've put all your energy into looking after your family and everyone else around you, and I had no idea that the loving, caring, funny Jo who has been there for us all was not as content as I imagined.*
>
> *Maybe my notes will help you, like me, to start putting yourself first?*
>
> *Chat soon!*
>
> *Love,*
>
> *Sam*
> *xx*

Jo read his notes and lists, surprised that she had never really realised how little life Sam had beyond his work at the hotel.

As she cooked dinner that evening, she kept mulling over the things Sam had written. His lists made sense, and his plans seemed to chart a logical path forward. Whether he could be as successful as he hoped, she wasn't sure, but she could see that not trying would leave him stuck in a dead-end job with no means of making the changes he wanted to make.

While the pasta was boiling, she sat down, picked up the phone, and dialled Sam's number.

'Hi, Jo!' Sam said cheerfully.

'Hi, Sam. Thanks for sending your lists over. I think they're really interesting.'

'And?'

'Well, they've given me a lot to think about.'

'In a good way?'

'Yes,' she said. 'I really liked them, and I think you should carry on looking at starting your own business. I think it would be a great step for you at this stage. You've got a plan, and I know you've got the skills to pull it off.'

'Thanks, Jo.' he said. 'That means a lot.'

'Can I ask you a favour?'

'What?'

'Would you mind if I copy them to use for myself?'

Sam laughed. 'Sure! Maybe we could compare notes when you've got your own lists?'

'That would be great! I've got to get dinner on the table, but I'll talk to you soon!'

'Great. Bye!'

Later that night, Jo sat and thought about the dreams she had had at university.

Before she had met James, she had completed her degree in art and design and spent a year travelling. She had experienced many different cultures, collecting ideas and samples with thoughts of one day starting her own interior design business. When she'd returned home, Jo had managed to secure a position with a top design company and started making a name for herself.

When Jo had met James, she'd known he was the man for her. Within a year, they were engaged and twelve months later, they were married and in their first home. A year after that, Jo had become pregnant, and they'd quickly been whirled into the next stage of their lives.

Jo's original plan of returning to work or starting her own business after Cassie went to nursery had had to be put on hold again when she became pregnant with Jack. And then James had started his architect firm, and her children had constantly seemed to need her to be at home. Cash and time were both too short for her to look into beginning a business, and she had loved being a mother.

Even now, with one child at university and the other college-age, her free time was limited. Being only part-time at James' firm meant she did most of the household chores.

With the COVID-19 pandemic, she was also now in charge of shopping for her parents, collecting their medication, and checking in on James's parents. James's sisters didn't seem too concerned about running errands for their parents, and there didn't seem much point in sending James on a separate mission when she was already going to the shops herself.

Jack studying from home instead of being in classes all day seemed to only add to the mountain of chores. Dirty plates from a dozen snacks were often piled up in the kitchen, with food left out on the counters, mugs scattered all over the place, and books and stationery strewn across the house. Some days, Jo felt lucky if she could find time to read a chapter of her bedtime novel before she fell asleep.

It was frustrating, she realised, so she sat down and began to copy some of the headings from Sam's notes. It soon became clear that she had not been following her own route for a long time. She had somehow taken on the role of supporting others at her own expense.

Next to Sam's lists, she scribbled a quick list of the things she usually did in a day, and then ticked off how many of them were things she did for herself, and how many were done for the sake of others. It was an eye-opening moment.

She had been a loyal daughter, a supportive wife, a caring mum, and a helpful friend, but who and what was 'Jo'? She had too many boats tied to her own to feel like she knew anymore.

She began to think about what she could do for herself, but nothing immediately came to mind. Her old dreams were long gone, her interior design skills out of date. She knew that she wanted to do something creative, but what? And how would her family cope if she wasn't running around after them all the time? That, she realised, might be the first problem to overcome.

When she looked at her lists, however, she knew she did need to overcome it. She couldn't spend every waking minute of every day making other people's lives easier. She had to take a few moments for herself. It was time for her to reconnect with the Jo she used to be, the Jo who had been full of hopes, dreams, and plans for the future.

Sharon and Viv – Our Journey cont'd ...

Having shared our dream of producing *Row Your Own Boat*, we now had to make the dream a reality.

We were aware that in the development stages, we would need to invest a lot of time, money, and effort into both our book and the supporting website if we wanted to reach our destination.

We also needed to ensure our work-life balance was maintained, as we both had other interests and family responsibilities, and we were not planning to neglect those.

Below are our responses to some of the questions asked in this chapter:

- What would our definition of success be? What is our dream?
  To be successfully running our own business – one that helps people to achieve their 'best life' and allows us to do the same.

- What would we like to accomplish?
  We'd like our book and website to help people identify where and how their lives can be improved, and for them to share their achievements so that, in turn, they can motivate others.

  We would like to develop a community of Row Your Own Boat rowers who can help and motivate each other (with our guidance and support).

- What could we do to make our lives better, to feel satisfied?
  To be working for ourselves in roles that we love and value, while being able to have a greater work-life balance.

- At the end of our lives, what is the one regret we **do not** want to have?
  That we did not try to pursue our dream, that we didn't step into our boats, pick up the oars, and start rowing.

- Out of all our wishes and dreams, which ones are the most important to us?
  Our desire to help and support others, enabling them to help themselves work towards having a better life.

- What can we do to make ourselves feel proud?
  Have our book released, get the supporting website and social media groups up and running, and see our fellow rowers find value in what we have to offer.

There may never be a perfect time to start a new venture, but perhaps when the world was in a middle of a pandemic, the circumstances were less than ideal. However, we both felt that although the country was struggling, it was the right time to start writing the book and developing the website. We wanted to be ready for when all restrictions were lifted and 'normality' was restored.

We realised that there would be a lot of people who had spent time during the lockdown examining their lives and looking for ways to either be happier or to be better prepared for the future. We wanted to be ready to offer them our help and support in achieving this. At this stage, nothing was going to hold us back.

We began by looking at what we had to do to reach our destination and how we were going to get there.

We set ourselves the following goals to keep us on track:

Time Frame	Objective
6 months	***Book ready to be submitted to an editor and sent out to a select group of readers to obtain feedback.***
12 months	***Book ready for release.*** ***Website under development.*** ***Training courses to be written and introduced.***
18 months	***Book on sale, website up and running with courses, workshops, and support groups, and some income generation.***
2 years	***Success stories coming in through our community of rowers, who will be helping each other, with our support. When COVID-19 is no longer a threat to everyday life, to be holding events and conferences to promote Row Your Own Boat and to share knowledge, experiences, and success stories.***

5 years ***Our book and website to continue to develop and grow with the business.***
To have produced a follow-up book and be running special events to support our rowers.
To have recruited staff to cope with the extra workload, who can bring their own experiences and skills to the company, as well as enabling us to achieve the work-life balance we're looking for - living our best life!

So, what did we need to change?

To enable us to reach our destination, there were several things we needed to change or improve on. We discussed these at length and came up with the following:

Our health – We needed to be ready and doing our best to make sure our boats were seaworthy. This included:

- ***Improving our overall health and fitness by improving our diets, reducing our weight, and taking up or increasing exercise***
- ***Reducing and managing pain***

Mental well-being – As well as making sure our boats were physically up to the journey ahead, we also needed to make sure our mental health was up to the challenge. We knew there could be times ahead when we might doubt if we could reach our destination. At these points, we'd need to draw on our inner strength and keep on rowing.

We decided we both wanted (and needed) to:

- ***Take responsibility for our own lives rather than being influenced by others***
- ***Focus on the positives***
- ***Enjoy life more***
- ***Learn how to handle stress better***
- ***Follow creative talents and try new things (perhaps take up a new hobby)***
- ***Have new adventures (step out of our comfort zones)***

Relationships – This was not a journey we would be taking on our own. We were in our own boats, but we would still benefit from having our friends and family cheering us on, supporting us through the storms and sharing our successes.

We both felt we had to:

- ***Deal with and move on from previous bad relationship experiences***
- ***End any poor or draining relationships***
- ***Find or further develop loving relationships with family and friends***
- ***Be more social and attract and accept new people into our lives***

Career – This was a new venture for us both and we both had to continue in our day jobs at first – we were not in a position where we could afford to leave. We had to continue giving 100% to our jobs while using our free time to work on our new venture.

We identified that we needed to:

- ***Manage our time carefully to fit in writing the book, etc.***
- ***Become more productive***
- ***Improve our existing skills (plus maybe acquire new ones?)***
- ***Network to develop opportunities***

Financial – This was an area we needed to monitor closely as neither of us had any experience of handling company finances.

We identified that we needed to:

- ***Learn new skills in accounting and bookkeeping***
- ***Set up and follow a budget***
- ***Research financial opportunities and best values***
- ***Negotiate with suppliers to obtain the best deals***
- ***Start saving or investing***

We also discussed offering additional products and services, such as employing guest speakers to appear at our live events.

Having worked our way through these sections, we now had a clearer destination in view and felt ready to start plotting our course.

We also defined our mission statement:

Our mission is to make a difference by inspiring, guiding, and empowering individuals to create a fulfilling everyday life in which they can thrive.

Chapter 3 – Plot Your Course

Row, row, row your boat,

Steady as can be,

If you don't plan it right,

You might get lost at sea.

In this chapter we cover:

- How to plan your route
- Effective goal setting

"I keep six honest serving-men

(they taught me all I knew):

*Their names are **What** and **Why** and **When***

*And **How** and **Where** and **Who**."*

Rudyard Kipling

Now is the time to start plotting your course.

Some questions that might help you to plan your journey include:

Where am I starting from?

What is my idea of success?

Who has succeeded before me?

How or **Why** did they manage to succeed?

When will I succeed?

Planning might seem a bit daunting, but if you use a diary, a to-do list, work targets, or even if you simply make lists before you go grocery shopping, then you already know how to plan.

Begin by going back over your dreams, hopes, and wishes list in the previous chapter.

You need to chart a course.

There are lots of systems you could use to help you organise your thoughts into a workable plan. The simplest is to grab a pen and some paper. On separate sheets, write down each aspect of your life that you would like to improve. Next, put the papers on a flat surface somewhere you can see them all. You can also do this with sticky notes.

For a more sophisticated method, you could search the internet until you find a planning method you feel comfortable with. A lot of them are free, so it's worth having a look for one you like.

Another well-known method is mind mapping. Again, this uses a pen and paper, but you put everything on one sheet. It can help you to organise your thoughts, record knowledge, and create and remember ideas.

To start your first mind map, draw a picture of yourself or your boat in the centre of a blank page. Next, add all the things you would like to do in bubbles around it (yes, all of them!). When you've done the first round, you can go back and add more items under each item you've noted.

For example, under HEALTH, if you want to lose or gain weight, draw new lines from the WEIGHT bubble and add more bubbles to show what you will need to do to make the changes you want to make.

Mind Map Example

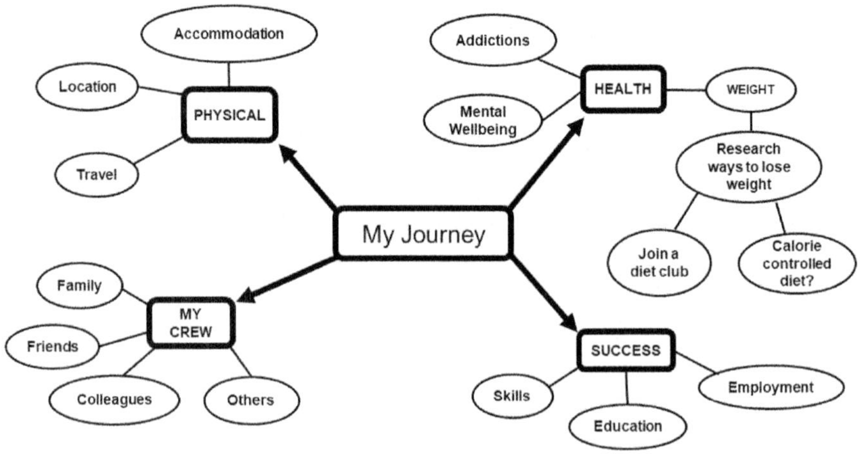

Now look at your goals and decide which is the most important.

Is there any one thing you really, really, really want to do, or to change, in your life?

Everything on your list may seem important, but if you try to tackle them all at once, you'll just confuse and demotivate yourself, so we suggest that you try to pick the things you feel are the most important first.

What is at the top of your list? Have you got an idea of where and how to start? Is there anything you need to do, learn, or prepare before you can begin?

Be sensible here; you want to improve your life, so which one thing on your list will give you the most help in moving towards your long-term goal?

You might not reach your tropical island paradise with this first voyage, but if it helps you to set off, that's an improvement on where you are now.

Once you've settled on your initial goal, decide how to work towards it to complete the first leg of your journey.

Think about every possible action which might help you to achieve your goal and make a note of each one. Include all the things you may need (e.g. information, cash, time, equipment, help, training, etc.).

You might also want to create an 'obstacles' list, considering problems that you may encounter, and how you might be able to solve them (e.g. health issues, financial constraints, etc.).

Do any need to be dealt with before you set off?

At the end of this activity, you might have a lot of things jotted down, but you should know exactly what you want to do, and what you need to do as a first move.

Don't fall into the trap of trying to set too many goals at once – if you do that, you could overwhelm yourself and you won't be able to work towards any of them consistently.

Many people fail to achieve their goals because they don't accurately define what needs to be done to achieve them. So once you know what you need to work on, you need to create a step-by-step detailed plan for each goal you have, this will help to change your mindset and help you feel more positive about the future.

You may have heard about SMART targeting:

S	**Specific**	Goals must be specific in order to be effective.
M	**Measurable**	Define the goal so you can measure your results.
A	**Achievable**	There's no point in setting an unachievable goal.
R	**Realistic**	If a goal is unrealistic, you will give up.
T	**Time-based**	Without a target date, you could flounder.

Plan and write your first goal using SMART targeting. The template below may help.

Specific	What am I going to do?
Measurable	How will I know when I have reached my goal?
Achievable	Is it achievable?
Realistic	Is it realistic?
Time-based	When will I achieve it by?
MY GOAL	
S	
M	
A	
R	
T	

Don't fall into the trap of making your targets too easy or too hard. You need to set targets that will take you away from where you are now, but not ones that are so challenging you'll lose your motivation.

Close your eyes and imagine yourself when you've made the change, or when you've achieved the first step towards it.

This is now going to be your life vision for the foreseeable future, whether that's a few weeks, a few months or even a year or two.

At this point, you can also decide on a reward system for yourself. It doesn't have to be big – dinner at a local restaurant, a new outfit, a day out, a weekend away, anything you feel is suitable to recognise your achievement and motivate you to carry on to the next part of your plan.

Rewards are an important part of keeping yourself moving forward, but it's also crucial to really commit to your new journey and decide that you are going to succeed.

If you carry on with just the vague intention of doing something at some time in the future, you know (as well as we do) that you'll never do it.

Only you can decide what you want, plan for it,

and then follow it through.

You must commit yourself to your voyage.

Plot your course, plan your steps, and then apply yourself.

Work at it.

Yes, it may well be hard, but if you genuinely want something, it will be worth it.

You **CAN** achieve your true desires.

You **CAN** live the life you want to live.

You **CAN** be the person you want to be.

Now, pick a date to start working towards your goal.

Put it in your diary or write it on a calendar and put it where you'll see it every day.

Decide how much time you can spend working on your goal – how many days per week or month, and how many hours per day. Next, you can start plotting target dates for specific steps.

Make sure you don't overstretch or stress yourself out by not allowing enough time for each item. Equally, don't allocate too much time; you may find you start to lose momentum.

You now have a definite plan for your future – a map of your voyage across the ocean of your new life.

Always remember:

> If you **DON'T** go after what you want, you'll never get it.
>
> If you **DON'T** ask for something, the answer will always be no.
>
> If you **DON'T** move forward, you will stay where you are.

As a final note in this chapter, you might find it helps to look at the changes not simply as doing something new or being different, but also as undoing the things in your life you're not happy with.

Think of it as unbecoming what you've been to date and reinventing yourself.

> *To make a change, you've got to make a choice.*
>
> *Take a chance and go with it*

It's time to let the real you climb up from the hold and stand proudly on the deck as captain of your boat.

What was a dream is now a plan.

It's a chart, a map you can follow on your journey.

In the next chapter we will move on to taking the helm and launching your new, improved boat.

Sam's voyage cont'd… **May 2020**

Sam decided the first thing he needed to do was to improve his physical condition and get himself back into shape. After all, if he was going to follow a new route, he would need to be up to it.

He produced a SMART targeting plan:

Specific	*Lose weight*
Measurable	*20 lb. (1½ – 2 lb. per week) and 2 to 4 inches off my waist*
Achievable	*Hell, yeah!*
Realistic	*Yes, if I follow a plan*
Time-based	*Four months (16 weeks max.)*

I will:

- *Take advantage of the 1 hour per day out of the house to exercise.*
- *Buy and eat more fruit, vegetables, and salads, and have fewer snacks.*
- *Eat regular meals.*
- *Tackle jobs in the house and avoid binge-watching TV.*
- *Sign up for online workouts.*
- *Be kind to myself and have the occasional treat, but not every day.*
- *Write down my achievements in case I need motivation when I am struggling.*
- *Set time aside each day to think about my course and how I aim to reach my first target.*

Sam's First Objective:

Start date:	*Today*
Objective:	*To get fitter, healthier, and happier, ready to tackle the next stage of my journey*
Rewards:	*A takeaway meal every two weeks*

This simple act of writing his first targeted plan made Sam feel better. He also decided to keep a daily journal so he could jot down his progress and any ideas he had.

Sam's Second Objective – Running his own business:

While he was feeling so positive, Sam decided to start thinking about what changes he could make to give himself the work-life balance he needed.

He honestly believed he could put all his skills and experiences into practice and the more he thought about it, the more he liked the idea of becoming an events coordinator. He knew the middle of a global pandemic was not the ideal time to start a new venture, but at least he had the time to weigh it up, research it, and decide if it was the right course for him.

Sam began by drafting a ***Business Action Plan:***

1. *Develop an overview of my business with ideas for what I can offer that other planners don't.*
2. *Research competitors and the services they provide.*
3. *Phone or email contacts developed through work.*
4. *Research suppliers – local and national.*
5. *Set up a contact and suppliers' database or register.*
6. *Look at options to facilitate events or offer packages such as a 'party in a box.'*
7. *Consider website and marketing options.*
8. *Look into pricing and other costs e.g. insurance, accountants, etc.*
9. *Research legal requirements, e.g. GDPR, health and safety, etc.*
10. *Research online IT courses to upgrade skills to help prepare for the challenges ahead.*

Planning and researching the possibility of getting his own business off the ground energised Sam.

He soon realised that the key to setting up his business would be to have a group of suppliers who he could trust, people who would want to work with him to provide a quality service. Through working at the hotel, Sam had already developed good relationships with a variety of suppliers and specialists, he decided he would begin with them.

Sam also decided to use a new approach in planning this route and began by drawing a mind map.

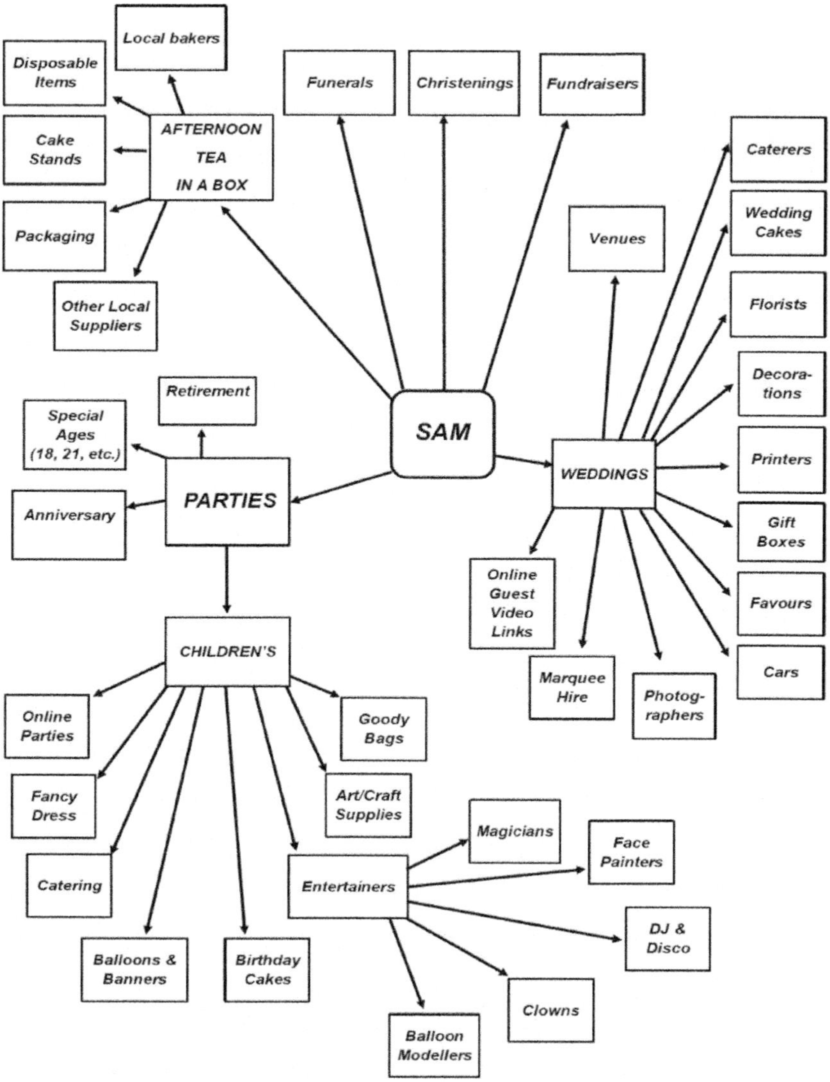

It took Jo a few days to write her lists and consider her future options. Like Sam, she knew she wanted more from life, but unlike him, she was not sure what she could, or should, aim for.

She wrestled with feelings of disloyalty; she had a good life, and she knew that to many looking in from the outside, she had nothing to be unhappy about. James worked hard and was generous. Her children were bright, healthy, funny, and caring. She was truly thankful for what she had, but like many wives and mums before her, she felt she had lost her identity. Her life was controlled by her family's plans and wishes, not her own.

Jo's first goal was to practice saying 'no.' She knew this would be hard, as everyone around her was used to her agreeing to anything they needed. Her parents often asked her to run errands for them, her children expected her to act as a chauffeur, cleaner, and personal chef, and even James tended to take her work around the house for granted, or hand her office work without any warning. She often found herself re-scheduling her whole day to fit in with what other people needed. It had to stop.

When Jo sat and thought about the things she did for herself, she soon realised that everything revolved around keeping her family happy. The only hobby she had for herself was reading, and she only had time for that when the kids were out or if James was working late. Jo needed to find a hobby for herself, something which would also allow her to tap into her creative skills. She wasn't sure where to start, but she began to make a list of a few dreams, hopes, and wishes.

With a new sense of purpose, she began the task of plotting the course to her Best Life, and being a 'list person,' she was in her element.

My Plan

1. *Go for my allowed daily walk and exercise at least four times per week at home (do online fitness classes?).*
2. *Practise saying 'no' and stick to it.*
3. *Talk to my family about how I feel and what I want to do.*
4. *Have a meeting with James and his sisters to discuss sharing responsibility for their parents' shopping, hospital appointments, etc.*
5. *Look at taking up a new hobby that would use my creative skills.*

6. *Have a regular date night with James?*
7. *Every week, pause to reflect on what I have achieved and what I still need to work on.*
8. *Write my bucket list!*

She decided to use a journal to record her progress and make notes about her thoughts and feelings as she moved ahead.

She also planned to start showing Jack how to be more independent by teaching him practical things like washing, cooking, cleaning, etc.

For Jo, the list was both empowering and frightening. For years, her life had centred on her family, their home, and their well-being. Now it was time for her to start taking her own needs into account and reconnecting with the Jo she used to be, so she could find the route to her best life.

At this point, she was not sure where her journey would lead, but she knew she needed to move to the next stage of her life.

Sharon and Viv – Our Journey cont'd…

Plotting our course

Having decided to get into our boats and row, it was vital that we planned exactly what we needed to do to reach our destination (getting our book published and our website up and running).

Our first meeting was mostly a brainstorming session. We were both so excited and full of ideas as to what our destination would include and what it should look like. The one thing that was clear at the outset was that we both had the same vision and reasons for undertaking this journey and we knew that together we would succeed, rather than going it alone.

We produced lists, mind maps (see one example below), and then even more lists – way too many to include here.

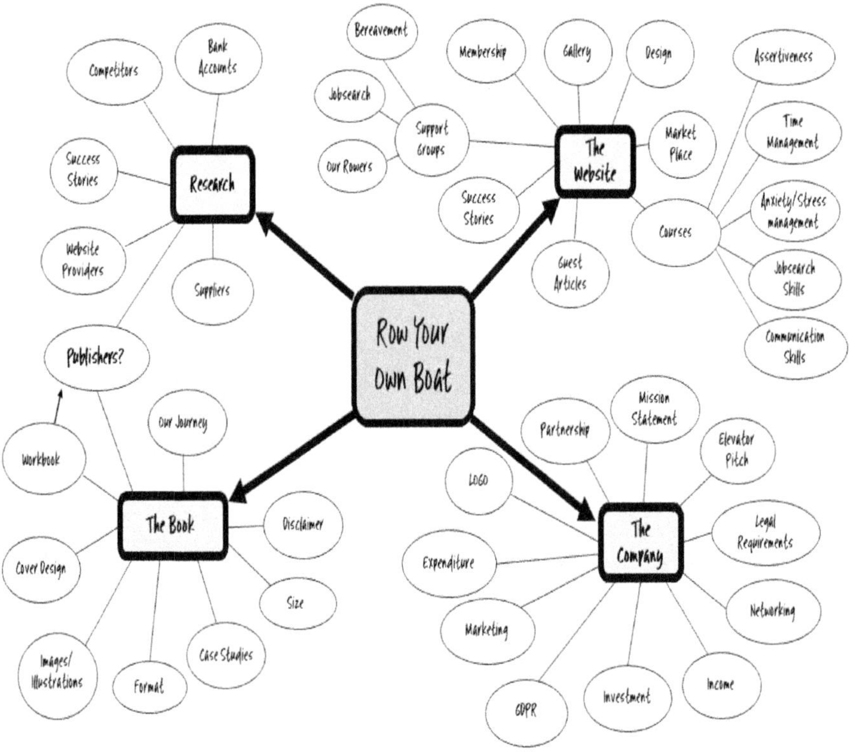

This meeting confirmed to us both that we had to concentrate on writing the book and avoid being distracted by other areas we would like to develop. We agreed to spend time thinking about the book and what the chapters would contain.

In the next planning session, we identified who we wanted the book to appeal to and what would make it different from every other self-help book. We listed the chapters and drafted the contents. We also agreed that for the time being, we would both have to continue in our day jobs. We recognise that this would slow our progress, but needs must!

By the end of the second session, we both had lists of tasks to complete. We agreed to keep in regular contact via telephone, video calls, and emails, and we also planned to meet weekly as we both needed the energy generated by our face-to-face sessions.

We acknowledged that there might be times when we couldn't complete everything on our to-do lists. As key workers, both with family responsibilities, it was important that we didn't put our own health and well-being at risk by trying to do too much. We were both keen to reach our destination, but we had to be realistic.

It was important for us to enjoy every aspect of our voyage, so nothing was written in stone. We acknowledged that given the climate we were working in (the pandemic), our plans might have to change, and that as the book and website developed, they might veer onto different courses than those planned. We would *'go with the flow'* and let our journey evolve.

With our boats, loosely tethered together, we picked up our oars and were ready to row and face whatever life threw at us.

PLAN = ***P****rioritise*

L*ist*

A*dapt and*

N*ever give up!*

Chapter 4 – Take the Helm

Rock, rock, rock your boat,

Steer it to and fro,

This way, that way, over the sea,

That's the way to go.

In this chapter we cover:

- Overcoming fear
- Bolstering self-belief
- The power of daily habits
- How to start moving forward

So if you've worked through the last chapter, you've now got a plan. You've defined your goals and charted the course you want to follow.

You've got your destination firmly in mind and you're ready to be captain of your own boat.

You may have spent years wishing, daydreaming, and hoping for a better future, and now it is time to act!

Time to take control, cast off the bowlines, row away from the harbour, feel the wind in your hair, the sun on your face, and head towards your destination.

> *There's no better day than today to step into your boat, pick up your oars and start rowing!*

You are the captain of your ship. All you have to do is take the helm and launch yourself off into your amazing future.

Except...

Here you are, at the quayside, staring blankly into space.

You are hesitating, frozen to the spot. Suddenly, it's all too much and you just can't bring yourself to set off.

What is stopping you?

FEAR!

Perhaps you're not just afraid; perhaps you are absolutely petrified.

Your mind is probably working flat out to find reasons that mean you will fail to achieve even the smallest of goals. It tries to talk you out of it. It makes you question everything, until you become scared of stepping into your boat and taking hold of the oars, let alone rowing into the future. Every bad scenario will pass through your mind – the possibility of being adrift on your own, of falling overboard during storms, and of being at the mercy of sea monsters or pirates.

But what are you really afraid of?

We all have fears, but the fear of change is one of the most powerful. Fear stops so many people from achieving their dreams.

Change is scary. Even if you know that you're making positive changes for yourself, it can be challenging. It's even more so when you're aware that setting out on your new journey could hurt not only yourself but others.

What you've got to ask yourself is what will hurt more in the long-term – staying somewhere which is **not** where you want to be, or making the changes that will take you to where you **do** want to be?

Look back at your life voyage to date.

What has your fear been holding you back from? Think of all the things you've missed out on because you were too scared to do what needed to be done, to change the things you needed to change.

What was stopping you?

What were you waiting for?

- The right time or circumstances?
- Other people to help?
- Some kind of miracle?

Most of us have learned that nothing in life is free and that if you want something, you have to work for it. A genie is not going to pop out of a bottle and give you your heart's desires; you have to man the boat and sail your course yourself.

You know that you must take responsibility for what you do, or don't do, to make your future what you want it to be. You have to overcome your fears!

This book will help you to find the way, but you need to do the work yourself, by yourself, and for yourself. No one else is going to come along and do it for you. If you are so afraid of failing that you don't even make a start, all of your dreams, hopes, and wishes will stop right here.

You might as well put this book down, forget everything you've read and worked on in the last chapters, and carry on living your life as normal.

If you allow it to, your fear of failure will lead to absolute failure.

So many wishes die with people who never got any further than hoping, dreaming, and planning. So many were not brave enough (or focused enough) to take the helm and push off out into the world, steering their preferred course.

Do you want to be another one of these people?

Do you want to spend the rest of your life wondering what might have been?

When you are lying on your deathbed, will you be wishing you had done the things you hoped for and dreamed of, the things you planned in the previous three chapters?

Will you be regretting that you weren't brave enough to do them?

Or will you look back with satisfaction, happy in the knowledge that you found the strength to follow through?

There is value in fear, but right now, at this point of your journey, the only fear you should allow yourself to experience and embrace is the fear of feeling regret if you do not pursue your dreams.

Take a moment to examine your fear. Can you feel it, really feel it, both physically and mentally? Explore the sensation and note down your thoughts.

This may be hard, but try to turn your fear into a positive thing.

Look at it from another angle; perhaps it's giving you the energy to overcome your challenges and make the changes you need to make. Maybe it's increasing your awareness of your situation or helping you to avoid unnecessary risks.

Fear can be a good thing if you embrace it!

Don't let your fear stop you. It is a natural emotion which we all have, but you should not let it hold you back.

The past can be a heavy anchor.
We must let go of who we have been to
become who we are going to be.

Now is the time to stop waiting, hoping, and wishing your life away, and actually start doing. If you really want to set off on your new voyage, you've got to be brave. You need to **stop** making excuses, **stop** inventing delays, and **stop** being scared.

Tying in with that, you have to start working on your self-belief. Whether we like it or not, our time on this Earth is limited, and many of us spend far too much of it doubting ourselves. None of us are guaranteed that time, so make it a mantra to never put things off until tomorrow if they could be done today.

You don't know if you'll reach your destination, but you need to feel that it's worth a try, and that you are worthy of trying. You are at the helm, you are the one making life better.

You aren't guaranteed success, but what's the worst that could happen?

Your journey is not about getting a chance: it's about making changes and taking the chances that arise from your actions. Your life won't change for the better until you adjust the way you do things and the way you look at everything and everyone around you.

Am I good enough?

Yes, you are!

How many ordinary people have done extraordinary things in their lives?

Look at people like J. K. Rowling (author), Marcus Rashford (footballer who campaigned for underprivileged children), and Sir Captain Tom Moore (who, at the age of 99, raised money for the NHS).

> *Few people succeed by accident.*
> *It takes hard work, commitment, and*
> *the desire to follow their dream.*

At some point in their lives, most successful people have probably felt like you do right now. If they succeeded, you can too, and it doesn't matter how simple or grand your goal is; your attitude will take you a long way towards it.

Stop talking down to yourself.

Part of self-belief involves stemming the flow of internal criticism. Many of us have spent years criticising ourselves, and we rarely even notice that we're doing it.

How often are you your own worst enemy?

Have you ever seen pictures of large animals tethered by small ropes that they could easily break? They don't because they have been conditioned to believe that they can't.

How many times have you told yourself that you cannot do something you'd like to do because you're not good enough, brave enough, clever enough, thin enough, young enough, or rich enough?

We say things to ourselves which we wouldn't dream of saying to someone else, so watch your thoughts, and if you catch yourself thinking anything which you would not be comfortable saying out loud to a friend, you need to pull yourself up and change that inner voice.

If you keep telling yourself that you're no good at something, you will come to believe it. If you've spent years criticising yourself or being criticised by others, it's going to be a hard habit to break, but now is the time to make a change and focus on the positives.

Every time you identify a damaging, critical thought, try to replace it with a positive one:

Examples of destructive 'self-talk'	**Examples of positive 'self-talk'**
I'm too stupid	I passed all my exams so I'm quite clever I am good with my hands
I don't stand a chance	I know I can do anything I set my mind to I don't know what I can achieve until I try
Sometimes I just hate myself	I like myself and I know others like me too
I'll never find a good job	Today is a new day, full of potential and opportunity
I feel like I'm too old/too fat/over the hill	I feel good physically, emotionally, and mentally I have years of experience
Nothing ever goes right for me	I am grateful for all that I have
Today is going to be awful	I can make today a great day
I have failed before, so I'll probably fail again	Just because I've failed in the past doesn't mean I'll fail again in the future

Sometimes, the negativity in our thoughts stems from things that have happened in our past, so let's try an exercise to explore letting go of these.

Imagine this:

You are sitting in your boat in a harbour.

You can see a tiny island on the horizon, so you decide to go there.

You begin to row. The more distance you put between yourself and the harbour, the less visible it becomes.

When you reach the island, you look back for the harbour, but you can hardly see it, although you know roughly where it is.

You decide to move on and explore the island. When you reach the other side, you look behind you, but the harbour is no longer in sight.

Does that mean that the harbour does not exist? No, of course not. It was there when you left and it is still there; you just can't see it now.

For those of you struggling with issues from your past that are holding you back, try to look at those things as if they were the harbour.

Row away from the bad stuff and leave it where it belongs – far behind you.

Yes, memories may pop up now and then, but remember that they cannot hold you back.

The things you remember did happen, but they are behind you now. Like the harbour, they are out of sight and have no power over you.

Go back to your lists of achievements, skills, and personal qualities from Chapter 1, and see if you can add to it.

Take some time to review all the things you are good at. Every time you think of something you can do well, it will help you to feel more positive about your abilities in general.

If you need to, ask friends or family for input. They may view many of the 'ordinary' things you do as brilliant, even if you barely notice those things.

How many of those things can help you on your journey?

Are you finding this difficult?

Is looking at yourself something you've always struggled with?

Have other people ever said negative things to you?

Things like:

- Do you really want to do this?
- Aren't you happy as you are?
- Is it worth the risk?
- Isn't the Devil you know better than having to face a new one?
- Are you sure you want to take the risk at your age?
- Aren't you afraid it won't work out?
- Won't that cost too much?
- What if it all goes wrong?

We'll examine their motives more thoroughly in the next chapter, but what do you think made them say those things?

Again, the answer is usually FEAR – they are probably afraid that if you better yourself, you might outgrow them. They want to keep you close by and don't want you to rock their boats, because then they'll have to make changes which they may find uncomfortable too.

If you have issues with confidence, their words might have a big impact.

You need to rise above them, but how?

IMPROVE YOUR SELF-ESTEEM

Self-esteem is the value you place on yourself. It's your opinion of your worth as an individual. We base this on our beliefs regarding our competence and whether we feel important, likeable, or successful.

You may suffer from low self-esteem – many people do – but your self-esteem is not fixed in place. It can be raised, but it is often hard to maintain and easy to lose.

We need positive self-esteem if we are going to row our own boats and succeed in life.

Look at the following chart and highlight where you see yourself:

People with high self-esteem	People with low self-esteem
Have a positive outlook and emotions	Are negative under most circumstances
Are happy and satisfied	Are not happy or satisfied
Look for self-improvement activities	Do not attempt self-improvement due to fear of failure
Are usually less anxious and take more risks in life	Worry about life and do not like taking risks
Recognise their successes	Do not recognise their successes
Try new ideas and take responsibility for their failures	Cannot face taking responsibility for their failures so they do not attempt new things
Usually feel equal to others	Believe they are inferior to others

Your appearance can also influence the way you feel. Stand tall and hold your head up, ready to meet the world head-on. Your outward look, the way you dress, and your personal grooming tell others a lot about you, but can also change the way you feel about yourself. Keep your body clean, your appearance tidy and appropriate, and dress to feel your best – and you will.

Even if you feel sad, make a point of smiling at and acknowledging others. Repetition will make it a habit and the act of smiling stimulates the happiness part of your brain, so you will feel better. It will also have a positive impact on the person you are smiling at!

REMOVE CLUTTER

Your well-being can be seriously affected by your physical environment. If you are living or working in a cluttered space, it will be harder to stay focused and work well.

A clean and tidy home or a nicely organised office is essential to maintaining your general well-being and motivation.

You could begin by sorting out and throwing away any old or unnecessary paperwork. In your pantry, dispose of out-of-date food or donate items you won't eat. If that seems too daunting, choose just ten things in the home that you don't use. Get rid of them. Next week, get rid of another ten.

Donate things to charity shops or sell them and use the money to improve your journey.

If you're surrounded by stuff that you no longer use or enjoy, ask yourself, *'Why am I keeping it?'* If there's no good reason, get rid of it.

If you find it impossible to get rid of things, ask for help from friends or a specialist.

Physical clutter can be a breeding ground for bacteria and can easily lead to physical illness. It will certainly drag you down mentally.

You should also be aware of mental clutter. How much is going on in your head at once? How can you work in a cluttered mental space? We've all experienced repetitive thoughts, bad ideas, or obsessions with unhealthy relationships, but you need to make an effort to *'throw away'* these things too. Mental clutter can be draining and will rob you of your energy and focus.

You need to get your life and yourself organised. Start getting rid of the clutter in your work, home, and mental spaces.

> *Awesome journeys can start with small steps.*

You've plotted your route and got a course to follow.

You know what you need to do to begin your voyage; now you need to do it.

Start today. If you only do one thing on your list, it will still move you closer to your destination.

Refer back to your diary or notes, pick one thing you can do right now, and do it!

DAILY HABITS

Daily habits can make a big difference to your success or failure, so let's explore them.

Firstly, examine your current habits and see if there are any that are holding you back which could be changed or stopped. Next, consider:

1. Planning and undertaking one small step each day to further your journey.

2. Focusing on the positives and setting off in the right direction. Start each day by smiling at yourself in a mirror, knowing that you are following your course and that you will make the most of the day ahead.

3. Reminding yourself often that you are working towards a more fulfilling and happier life.

4. Avoiding detours – don't go out of your way or stop to pick up passengers unless you want to include them in your journey (there's more on this in Chapter 5 – Your Crew).

5. Smiling more; don't hang around with or listen to negative people.

6. Going to sleep earlier and getting up earlier.

7. Practising gratitude – yes, we know it's corny, but use a few minutes each day to practise gratitude for everything you can think of. Write these down or use an app. You can include many things,

such as family, friends, career, health, animals, the natural world. Be thankful for anything beautiful you notice, no matter how small. It will make you feel happier and more focused. Try it!

8. Learning something new every day. Read an article, look up a fact on the internet, or memorise a new word.

9. Leaving work at work.

10. Trying to stay in the present moment. Focusing on the past or fixating on the future is wasted effort. Only the present moment is real.

11. Taking time in the evening to evaluate and appreciate the progress you have made towards your goal. Keep your eye on the prize.

12. Recognising your emotions. You may not always feel happy and that's fine. We all have our bad days. If it's a one-off day, ignore it and it will pass. If you find more and more down days creeping in, consider getting some help (see Chapter 7 – Storms of Life).

You can also join us on social media, where you can find fellow travellers, shared experiences, and emotional support – we are at:

Facebook	@rowyourownboat21
Instagram	rowyourownboatonline

Full details can be found on our website: www.rowyourownboat.co.uk

If it all still seems too much, go back to the previous chapter and re-examine or even redefine your goals. Rewrite your notes accordingly. You may need to break things down into smaller, more manageable steps.

BUT

- Don't use fear as an excuse to keep putting off your start date.
- Don't dwell on past regrets. Previous failures show that you've been brave enough to try.
- If past issues are becoming a barrier, seek help from a counsellor.
- Face new problems head-on.
- Consider hiring a coach or taking a course to help you achieve your goals faster and with more focus.

If you want to live the life you've imagined and be free to spend your time however you like, you've got to go for it!

Pearls don't lie on the seashore;

if you want one, you'll have to dive for it.

Even if it is something you've been putting off for years, start by taking the first step (no matter how small) towards your goal, right now.

No more excuses. If you don't move forward now, you will stay exactly where you are forever, and possibly regret it until the end of your life.

Whatever is in your plan, start working towards it

DO IT NOW,

DO IT TODAY!

It might be your last chance to live the life you've always wanted.

It is time to take the helm,

row your own boat

and

follow the stars...

Sam's voyage cont'd... **June 2020**

Sam's goal to be healthier and happier got off to a good start.

During the lockdown, everyone was limited to only one hour per day out of their homes to exercise, so Sam volunteered to take his elderly next-door neighbours' dog, Bobby, out for a second daily walk. This helped to increase his stamina and gave him the chance to experience handling a dog.

Sam also wrote healthy meal plans for each week, so that he only bought the items he needed, rather than the treats he fancied. Sam began tackling the jobs in his house and garden, which had been neglected due to his long hours at work. To help keep himself motivated, he also made daily notes about what he had achieved and put these on his notice board in the kitchen.

Sam was surprised to find his confidence in himself was growing. He had always felt confident in his ability to do his job, but he was occasionally self-conscious and a little awkward outside of work. Now, when walking the dog, he would take the time to stop and chat (at a safe distance) with neighbours and other people out walking their dogs. Sam made a promise to himself that no matter where life took him in the future, he would always make time to chat with people along the way.

In the first week of June, Sam had a call from Jo.

'Hey, Sam. How's it going?'

'Great!' he answered. 'I'm feeling better than I have for ages. How are you?'

'I'm fine. You know how I loved all your notes and things? Well, I wondered if you'd like to meet up to chat about it all?' She paused. 'I've been working through my own answers to them too...'

'Brilliant!' he said. 'When were you thinking?'

'Well, we can meet outside now, so I thought next week. Maybe each bring a picnic lunch?'

'Great!' he said. 'It seems like forever since we saw each other.'

'I know! It's all been so horrible, hasn't it? I was thinking next Friday, at the park.'

'I'll look forward to it.'

'Me too,' she said. 'I can't wait to hear about what you've been doing, and I'd like to talk about a few ideas of my own.'

After her call, Sam thought about his plans. While his diet and exercise plan had gone well and he was now fitter, had lost weight and knew that he looked a lot better than before, his second goal had not got off to a good start. Every day, he told himself he would start planning his business ideas, but there was always something more important to do – a cupboard to sort out, a lawn to mow, shopping to finish. Now Jo was expecting him to tell her all about his new business and he had nothing.

He realised that for some reason, he had been avoiding starting. Why was that? Was it a fear of failure, or simply a fear of making the changes he knew he would have to make?

Sam looked at his notes and went back to the beginning. He was reminded of his hopes and dreams, and of the progress he had made with his health. He was much happier with his physical and mental state now, but there was so much more he wanted to do with his life.

Sam took another look at his skills and qualities, at all the things that made him suitable to run an events business. He knew, given his experience and abilities, he had 'nothing to fear but fear itself.'

Despite his confidence in his ideas, Sam felt he needed a sounding board, somebody who would listen to his ideas without putting him down or dismissing them. He would be honest with Jo and ask for her opinion at the picnic.

In the meantime, he would do as much as possible to plot the course towards his events business. He settled down for the afternoon and began to carry out some research, list his potential contacts, and think about what the business would involve.

Since writing her lists, Jo had made time to exercise every day. She went for her permitted hour-long walks around the neighbourhood and later, when it was announced that people could exercise more than once per day, she began to visit her local parks.

These walks gave Jo a chance to see her area in a new light. She noticed how each house was different, how their gardens varied and reflected the personalities of the people who lived there. She took the time to chat with her neighbours and began to reconnect with the town she had lived in for years.

Jo started to take photos on her phone and surprised herself with the quality and composition of her images. She began taking her camera out on her walks and captured images of anything which appealed to her. Soon, photography became a hobby that not only helped her to stay fit, but also gave her an outlet for her creative side.

Another bonus of the daily walks was that Jo began to chat with other walkers, especially those out walking their dogs. Some of them seemed lonely, and Jo – well aware of how lucky she was to have a loving family in her home – took personal satisfaction in being able to brighten their days.

She also found that she loved watching the dogs playing together or chasing after sticks or balls around the park. She began to ask if she could photograph them, and most of the owners were more than happy, especially when she offered to email them copies of her photos. She got a lot of complimentary replies.

Jo started to make changes in other areas too. She began to spend more quality time with her parents, sitting down in the garden for tea, cakes and conversation.

Having always thought of her parents as Mum and Dad, she decided she needed to get to know them as Rose and Derek, so she made a point of asking about their memories, their early lives, how they had met, and what their hopes and dreams had been. These conversations provided a major boost to their relationship, and she came to view her visits not just as seeing her parents, but also as meeting friends.

Jo began to write down the stories her parents shared with her. She borrowed some of their old photographs on the pretext of making copies for the kids – but in reality, she was thinking of making a present for their 50th wedding anniversary, which was only a year away.

She asked James for help to make their special anniversary memorable for them, and he seemed pleasantly surprised and pleased to be asked.

'What were you thinking of?' he asked.

'I don't know,' she said. 'I thought we could surprise them with a holiday. I thought maybe you could book one.'

'Are you sure you want to leave it to me?'

Jo nodded. 'I'm collecting photos and things to put into an album for them, but if you could find a nice holiday to give them, it would be one less thing for me to think about.'

James beamed at her. 'OK, I'll start looking and see what I can find.'

'I know they'll be pleased that you've been involved with it.'

At the end of each week, Jo looked at her list and marked off anything she felt she had achieved. She was making good progress, but when she looked at the things left to do, she noticed a pattern; the things she had yet to tackle were those that made her nervous. They involved having difficult conversations with other people, especially conversations about them taking more responsibility for themselves and becoming less reliant on her.

It might be hard, but she was determined. If she was going to keep doing the new things she was enjoying, she needed to tackle her obstacles head-on.

It was time that James and his sisters, Megan and Beth, did their fair share of caring for their parents. Jo was happy to help when it was genuinely needed, but she was no longer prepared to be the automatic choice for all of their errands.

She also needed to talk to James and Jack about sharing the chores at home and not leaving everything in the house for her to do.

At the beginning of June, she called Sam and asked him to meet her for a picnic. She knew he would give her his opinion on some of her thoughts and plans, and she was interested to see what he had been doing.

The following Friday, Jo settled at a picnic table in the local park, and soon spotted Sam striding over with a dog bouncing at his side. Already, she could see the changes in him; he looked healthier than he had for ages, and definitely happier.

'Oh my God, look at you,' she said. 'You look so well! What have you been doing?'

Sam sat opposite her. 'Well, I never sent you the weight loss part of my plans, but in the end, I picked that as my top priority – to get a bit healthier. And I've stuck at it,' he said cheerfully.

'Well, it certainly looks like it!' Jo smiled. 'How are the rest of your plans going?'

'Well, you know I was thinking about starting my own business.' He smiled back. 'I might go into event management when this pandemic's behind us.'

'That's exciting, what are you thinking?'

Sam spent the next ten minutes outlining the ideas he was considering and the tentative plans he had made.

Jo listened with interest. 'Organising events would be so good for you. You've been wasted managing that reception. I think it would be perfect,' she said. 'You should go for it!'

'Thanks Jo, that really means a lot.' he said. 'How are you getting on? You said you were having a go at your own notes?'

'Yes, I've drawn up a plan too. Could you have a look at it?'

Sam nodded, 'Yes, no problem!'

Jo reached into her bag for a copy which she handed to him.

'How's it going so far?'

'Really well. I'm exercising more and have taken up photography. I'm writing in a journal every week to keep track of what I've done, so it's coming along.'

Sam scanned her notes. 'And what about the other things? Have you started them?'

'Not yet,' Jo shook her head. 'Some of them aren't so easy.' She hesitated. 'Talking to the family might be difficult. I've been planning what I could say but I need to wait for the right moment.'

Sam gave her a wide grin. 'Why don't you rehearse them with me now?'

They spent the next few minutes discussing Jo's issues with her family and how she could raise them without upsetting anyone.

The rest of their lunch passed quickly. Jo enjoyed herself, and took lots of photos of Bobby.

'I've loved doing this throughout lockdown,' she said, waving the camera.

'Why don't you think about doing something with that then?' he suggested.

'What do you mean?'

'I don't know, maybe do a photography course, and then offer to do portraits of everyone.'

She grinned. 'That's a lovely idea but I'm not good enough, or confident enough, to do people yet.' She checked the image previews on her camera's screen. 'I'm getting pretty good with animals, though.'

She passed the camera to him.

Sam scrolled through the images. 'Jo, these are fantastic! Can you email them to me? Bobby's owners would love them.' He looked at her. 'You really should think about it. If you like photographing animals, why don't you contact the animal shelter? They might need someone to do photos to put on their re-homing site.'

Jo paused. 'That's a great idea! I'll look into it.'

When she got home, Jo wrote notes about Sam's suggestion in her journal, looked up the local shelter's contact details, and added, ***'Contact the animal shelter to see if I can get involved with their fundraising'*** *to her plan.*

With a new sense of purpose, Jo invited her sisters-in-law to a barbecue at the end of the month. Cassie would be home for the summer then too, so it would be a chance to get everyone together.

Although she felt nervous about telling everyone what she wanted to change, now the obstacles blocking her route did not seem to be so daunting.

Sharon and Viv – Our Journey cont'd...

Fear had, in the past, stopped both of us from getting in our boats, picking up the oars, and rowing towards our destinations, but we were determined that would not happen on this journey. Working together made it easier for us both.

We knew that the journey might not be plain sailing, that there could be storms ahead, and that our plans might have to be changed, but we also knew that having each other for support would give us the strength and courage to keep rowing and not give up.

Having this common goal didn't mean we would always be in the same place. We were aware that we would disagree sometimes, and that at points, one or the other of us might have doubts and question our course. At times, we've both wondered:

- Are we doing the right thing?
- Are we up to the challenge ahead?
- Are we ever going to reach our destination?
- Should we stop, row back to shore, and abandon our boats?

It was at these times we needed to be honest and share how we were feeling so we could be there for each other. Low self-esteem can be a barrier to achieving so much and if either of us found ourselves doubting our ability, the other one would reassure them of their true worth.

At our age, we have both accrued a lot of *'stuff,'* both physical and emotional. To take the helm and keep rowing, we needed to declutter, clear the decks, and focus on the journey ahead. We decided to start by organising our home office spaces and throwing out all the outdated training materials we had produced over the years.

Our energy was divided between our day jobs, *Row Your Own Boat*, and our personal lives, so maintaining our work-life balance was a challenge. Because we were both working hard during the pandemic, we knew that *Row Your Own Boat* might progress slowly at times. We decided to stay positive, focus on our destination, and remember that by working together, we were working towards our dreams.

Chapter 5 – Your Crew

Row, row, row your boat,

Gently down the stream,

Throw those stowaways overboard,

And listen to them scream.

In this chapter we cover:

- Whether you need a crew and what purpose a crew serves
- What makes a good captain
- How to manage crew relationships
- How to respect yourself

Having worked your way through the first four chapters, the next stage is to decide whether you are going to sail solo or if you need a crew.

Is rowing your own boat something you need to do for yourself? Is sailing solo going to be a key part of your journey, a challenge in itself, or do you want or need the help and support of those around you? If so, who will be in your crew?

Your crew could be partners, family, friends, work colleagues, associates, tradespeople, professionals or anyone who can help you reach your destination.

These people could be cheering you on from the shore, rowing alongside you, or in your boat with you. They could also support you through hard times by giving your boat a tow, letting you ride in their boat, and even helping you with repairs.

Now ask yourself this question:

Do I need a crew?

If your answer is **NO** and you want to go it alone, here are some things you might want to consider:

Am I going to tell anyone about my plans to row my own boat or is this something I am going to do by myself, for myself?

For some of us who have never faced a challenge on our own, this could be the ideal opportunity to step into the boat and look forward to this new adventure. This doesn't mean we're turning away from our old life and those who love and care for us. It's just a chance for us to grow and find out who we are. The people around us may be pleasantly surprised by the results.

Should I tell those closest to me about my journey so that they can support me from the shore, cheering me on my way as I take the oars and set off on my course?

There are times in our lives when we all benefit from having someone in our corner cheering us on. It's not a sign of weakness, but only you will know if telling others will enhance your journey or detract from it. You may decide not to tell everyone in case it doesn't go to plan, but telling someone you trust, who will be honest and respect your journey, will give you someone to share your hopes and ideas with.

Do I need to look for others on the same journey so that we can support each other as we face whatever lies ahead?

Again, it's up to you, but there are plenty of benefits in doing so, and many ways to connect with others on the same route as you, depending on the path you are planning to follow. For example, if your goal is to lose weight and become healthier, joining a slimming club or a support group may be just what you need.

Strangers on the same journey may be able to offer more help and support than those around you who have never experienced what you are hoping to achieve. A friend who has never dealt with a weight problem but tries to offer you weight loss advice may have you running for the hills or the nearest bar of chocolate, rather than encouraging you to step into your boat.

Am I choosing to go it alone and not tell anyone because of my fear of failure?

If you don't get it right the first time, you don't need to be afraid – this isn't the end of the journey. It's just a setback. If you stalled your car on your first lesson, you wouldn't quit driving, would you?

When something goes wrong, use it as a learning curve, revisit your plans, and revise them if necessary. You may have to do this again and again, but as long as you never lose sight of your destination and you're enjoying the journey, nothing else matters.

If your answer was *'**YES**, I will need a crew,'* begin by looking at the people in your life. You may find that you've got the crew that you need already. Take the opportunity to share your plans with your potential crew and see if they want to help and support you on your journey. When they see the thought and planning you've put into reaching your destination, they might be eager to get involved.

To make sure you recruit the crew you need and not a crew you are forced to take, here are a few things to think about:

WHAT DO I NEED FROM MY CREW?

As with some of the previous questions, your answers will depend on the course you are planning to take.

Time

For those with children or other dependents, time is extremely valuable. Asking someone to help out with babysitting, the school run, etc., may not seem like much, but it will give you some free time to begin rowing your own boat.

Skills

Having assessed your boat in Chapter 1, you may be aware that you need to learn new skills or develop existing ones. This could include asking for help with your IT skills or managing your finances.

Financial Support

The amount of financial support you may need from your crew and what is available will depend on your personal circumstances and your plan.

If working to a budget is an area you struggle with, your crew may be able to help and support you with this by developing a savings plan with you or identifying areas to reduce your spending.

If your goal will include major changes to your income, (i.e. changing careers or setting up a business etc.) you will need to ensure that anyone affected by this is on board.

Emotional Support

For some people, emotional support is crucial. Having someone who will listen to your ideas and offer a balanced opinion and moral support when you are facing a storm at sea can be invaluable. This person needs to be honest, loyal, and trustworthy. You don't want to confide in someone who will broadcast your private conversations to the world or use the information to undermine your position as captain of the crew.

> *Asking for help from your crew is not a sign of weakness, but a sign of strength.*

WHO DO I NEED IN MY CREW?

While you've been looking at those around you, you may have noticed that there are a lot of people with their boats tied to yours, as well as those that are trying to hitch a ride in your boat. Now is the time to decide whether you should tighten the ropes or let them go.

You are probably already familiar with *'stowaways.'* These are the people who never call, who make plans without reference to your schedule, and who expect you to drop everything to help them without feeling they should do anything in return. These are the people you *do not want* in your boat!

Getting rid of them may be difficult, especially if you have granted them a free ride in the past. However, you need to be strong enough to get them to row their own boats just as you are rowing yours. While you don't want to hurt anyone, you should also respect yourself and your needs.

You may also realise that some people who you thought were your helpful crew members are, in reality, pirates. They will take everything they can from you, acting in their own interests and offering no support. These people are usually the ones who are particularly upset when you start to change your life, because it will threaten their ability to take advantage of you.

Remember that when stowaways and pirates get angry because you say no, it does not mean that you should have said yes.

Stand up for yourself!

Keep in mind that:

- If you have lots of boats tied to yours and nobody else is rowing, you will rapidly become exhausted.
- If all the boats are expecting you to row towards their destinations and not your own, you will soon grow resentful.
- If some of the boats are more powerful than others, they may try to control all the boats and there will inevitably be friction, or even a mutiny!

We're not saying that your journey should become all-consuming to the extent that you neglect your loved ones and obsess over it, but equally, it needs to be a defining factor in your life.

At times, the people around you or in your crew may need extra support from you, just as you may need help from them. If someone becomes sick or faces financial hardship, you may need to tie them alongside your boat or even take them into your boat to give them time to recover their sea legs. Be mindful that as soon as they are ready, they need to get back into their own boat; don't let the situation drag on for longer than is needed, even if you do feel sorry for them.

There's a lot of satisfaction in helping others, as long as this is not at the expense of your own happiness and well-being. Be mindful and keep a weather eye out for anyone who may be taking advantage of your situation and/or your kindness.

WHAT MAKES A GOOD CAPTAIN?

Before we talk about how to handle a crew, let's look at the qualities and skills that make a good captain. Are you going to be calm, assertive, open, honest, and ready to face any storms with patience and compassion, or are you going to let the crew take the lead, leaving you all at sea?

Identify which of the following fundamental skills and qualities you have and which you need to work on. It may be worth going back to Chapter 1 to look at your skills and personal qualities.

Vision

A good captain will look beyond today. They should have a vision of where they and their crew will be in the future. They will plan and take the time to review their progress (making any changes needed).

Optimism

A good captain must be able to motivate and inspire others, with an optimistic and upbeat attitude. They will focus on the positive side of things, adopting a hopeful approach that will help to encourage a 'can do' attitude in their crew.

Adaptability

A good captain will need to be ready to face whatever the voyage throws at them. As captain, you should not be afraid to change your plans if the current plan is no longer working. Remember to ask for your crew's input as you draft a new plan, especially if someone has specialist knowledge that will help.

Strong Communication Skills

A good captain must be able to explain their thoughts or ideas easily. They will communicate positively and calmly, be courteous and treat others as they would like to be treated.

They will also explain situations as they see them, openly, honestly and directly, without getting emotional or upsetting others. They will understand that communication is a two-way street. Listening to what your crew members have to say, really listening, is a crucial aspect of communication.

Confidence

A good captain must be someone their crew can believe in and trust. Confidence does not mean arrogance or putting people down. A truly confident person is simply aware of their abilities, knows what they are good at, and is not afraid of responsibility and pressure. They will take responsibility for their own actions and admit when they are wrong. A confident, assertive captain is what a crew wants when facing a storm.

Decisiveness

Decision-making is at the heart of captaincy. Captains must determine what course the crew should take, without being either too hasty or missing opportunities due to hesitation.

Few of us were born great captains, but as we discussed in Chapter 1, a lot of us have the qualities and transferable skills that, with continued development, will help us to become good captains.

If you feel that you are lacking any of these qualities or skills, now is the time to do something about it. Have a look online and see if you can find any courses which may work for you, or you could join a community or support group which could help.

MANAGING YOUR CREW

Every situation is different and how you deal with your crew will vary according to the circumstances. Every time you interact with a crew member, remember to show them respect (even if they don't return it).

There will be times when you need to support a crew member as they face a personal storm. This will help them become a better and stronger crew member, who could then offer help and support when you need it.

The hardest role you are likely to have to play as a captain will be letting go of crew members who are not pulling their weight, or pirates who are actively trying to scuttle the ship. This is an important aspect of crew management, even though it can be unpleasant.

To better evaluate your crew, look at the following chart and see which column your relationship with your crew falls under.

You may want to use a separate chart for each member of your crew.

Aspect	People in healthy relationships:	People in unhealthy relationships:
Equality	Share responsibilities and make joint decisions	One person makes the decisions and dictates to the other
Safety	Feel physically, mentally, and sexually safe in each other's presence	Use physical force, sexual coercion, or mental abuse to get their own way
Respect	Listen to each other and respect each other's opinions and personal belongings	Disrespect each other, talk down to or over each other, or destroy the other person's personal belongings

Honesty	Share information and concerns and listen to the other person's information and concerns	Disregard each other and lie to, steal from, or gossip about each other
Dependence	Do not depend on each other for their sense of identity	Are dependent on the presence of others and insist they cannot live without them
Comfort	Share enjoyable relationships, laugh together, have fun, and support each other when necessary	Do not have fun together, do not laugh together, and are never there when their support is needed

Hopefully, this chart will help you to see if the relationship with each crew member is healthy or unhealthy. If your relationships are healthy but you are still feeling uneasy, it may be down to your personal insecurities.

However, if you find that the 'unhealthy relationships' column applies to someone in your crew, it's a sign that you need to make a change. If you feel that someone is holding you back, they probably are.

It's time to take charge of your boat.

It may be hard to change the habits of a lifetime, but this is your boat and your journey, and you cannot let others control it.

At this point, you need to realise and accept that every human being has the right to defend their basic rights and you are not an exception.

Your basic human rights are not a wishy-washy dream. They exist.

Take a look at the following lists. Tick the ones you already live your life by and highlight any that you need to work on.

I have the right to:

- say no to demands
- be me and express all my feelings, whether positive or negative
- determine my own standards
- build and maintain a good life for myself

- make my own decisions and live my life the way I want to
- define and work on my own priorities
- have my needs and wants respected by others
- make friends and feel comfortable around people
- have my own private time and personal space
- live and work in a safe environment
- be angry with someone I love
- be mentally and physically healthy
- take chances
- make my own mistakes and learn from them
- receive honesty from others

As an individual, I am not:

- obliged to give excuses or reasons for my behaviour
- required to suffer because of others' bad behaviour
- responsible for other people's actions, feelings, or problems
- required to associate with people who deliberately or inadvertently:
    - abuse me mentally or physically
    - attempt to manipulate me
    - humiliate me
    - lie to me or about me

How many of these rights do you not insist on because you are too afraid of upsetting, infuriating, or alienating others?

We all, at some points in our lives, will put the needs and wants of others before our own. Some will do it more than others, and some of us do it all the time. When you count how often you do this, you may be surprised at how few of your rights you are living your life by.

There is consolation in the fact that you are not alone. Many of us find it hard to state our rights, and we stop putting our own needs first.

WHY?

Most of us want to be loved, and we're afraid that if we rock the boat, our crew will desert us.

If our crew provide most of our physical, emotional, or financial support, we may fear what our lives will become if we try to change them.

If your crew care for you, they will accept and respect your rights.

Of course, they may be surprised that you've decided to change things, especially if they are happy with the way things are.

They may feel insecure and threatened, but good communication should help you explain your plans and reassure them that they still have a role to play – even if they're simply cheering you on from their boat.

You can compromise when needed, but don't compromise your rights. Define your levels, stick to them, and respect other people's levels. Some people may accuse you of deserting them, of wrecking their ship and leaving them to drown, but stand your ground.

You cannot rescue people from their own attitudes and opinions.

Your purpose in life is not to save everyone.

You are not a lifeboat!

You can shine a light and show them the way, but you cannot save them, especially if doing so would hurt you or hinder your journey.

If your crew are not prepared to support you as you row towards your destination, you must go on alone and leave behind those who have treated you badly.

As soon as you realise that you need to row away from someone, be brave. Don't linger, simply hold your head up and go with dignity.

It's not selfish to want to improve your life.

Those who love and support you and who want you to succeed will either row beside you or follow on in your wake, but your life will become easier when you leave difficult crew members behind.

Nurture solid relationships with crew members who understand the voyage you are taking and support you all the way.

If you need support from someone else, try to find a *'First Mate'* to help. This could be someone who, like you, is trying to accomplish something. Offer your support in return for theirs and you can both encourage and motivate each other as you journey towards your goals.

If you don't know anyone at the moment, search for them on social media, or join community activities or local groups; there are plenty out there. Go to our website and see if there is a group of fellow rowers following the same course as you.

Nobody said rowing your own boat was going to be easy – we may have to face ripples or even a tsunami along the way – but remember that the day will arrive when you love yourself enough to say, ***'I deserve better than this'*** and mean it enough to take action.

> *Plan for it, believe in it, and then do it!*

Now, on the next page, draw a map of your ocean and plot your journey as a positive reminder of where you are now and what you hope to achieve.

My map, my plan, my journey:

Jo saying 'Go for it!' gave Sam a boost and being told he was wasted in his current job was exactly what he needed to hear.

After seeing Jo, Sam thought about the problems she had been having with the people in her life and began to look closely at the people around him. He realised that there were some people who only got in touch with him when they wanted something, or only talked about themselves. However, he also had loyal friends who were invested in him and his happiness as well as their own. When the pandemic was over, he decided, he would be more selective about who he spent time with.

Exercising had brought Sam a few new connections, and improved the quality of some of the old ones. A couple of colleagues from his hotel were walkers and throughout the summer, they were happy to meet with Sam to exercise.

One of Sam's new acquaintances, who owned a dog called Luke, was a specialist in web design, and talking to him as their dogs played in the park got Sam thinking about his journey and what Jo had said. 'Go for it!' was encouraging, but how could he do that if he didn't have any idea how to build a website or contact suppliers?

When Sam got home, he sat down and took out his business plans, and spent a bit of time identifying the areas where he knew he would struggle if he tried to go it alone. He wasn't sure who he was going to ask to help him, but just recognising he needed help was a start.

Sam drew up a list of the people he would eventually need:

1. ***Web designer/IT specialist -*** *Although Sam had reasonable IT skills, web design was outside his experience. He also recognised that he would need someone with a greater general IT understanding than his; he knew his own limitations.*
2. ***Legal Advisor -*** *Sam had no specialist legal knowledge, so here he would also need some help.*
3. ***Children's Party Advisor -*** *Sam had never had children and although he could do some research online, he would benefit from having advice from someone with experience.*
4. ***Suppliers -*** *Sam wanted to develop a list of suppliers he could trust and rely on to provide a quality product or service. He had high standards and would accept nothing else from those who worked with him.*

Jo was delighted when her daughter came home from university on 25th June. Cassie had not been home since February.

Jo cooked a welcome home meal and the family sat together chatting happily. When everyone had finished, Jo said, 'Now we're all together again, there's something I need to discuss with you all.'

James raised his eyebrows and Cassie and Jack gave her surprised looks.

'Don't worry, it's nothing bad,' Jo said. 'Although there's something important that I need to tell you.'

'Go on,' James said quietly.

'I don't know how to start...' Jo trailed off for a moment, steeling her nerves.

'Um... basically, well... I'm not very happy.'

'Why? What's happened?' Cassie asked.

'It's hard to explain, but I've been looking at my life, at all our lives, and I've realised that I need to do more things just for me.'

'Good idea, Mum,' Jack said.

'What do you want to do?' James asked.

'I haven't made a definite decision about anything long-term, but I'm thinking about doing something with photography. You know I've been taking a lot of pictures when I've been out and about, and I love animals, so I've spoken to the animal shelter, and I've volunteered to take photos of the ones they need to find homes for. If they're good enough, they'll put them on their website.'

'Wow!' said Jack.

'What a lovely idea.' Cassie beamed. 'That's so sweet!'

'But I need you all to help me.'

'How?' James asked.

'I need more help around here. When you're here, you're all happy to leave everything in the house for me to do, and I just can't do it anymore.' Seeing their stunned faces, she added, 'I know it's hard to make changes, but I

think you are all capable of helping me a lot more than you do. I know it's partly my fault for not telling you how I felt before now, but I can show you how to do all the things I do. I mean, Jack, you are more than old enough to do your own washing and clean up after yourself.'

Cassie grinned at her brother, 'Better to learn to be self-sufficient now, before you go to uni.'

'I suppose,' he grunted.

'What about work?' James asked.

'Nothing will change there. I think that if I have the time to do this, to do something for me, I'll be much happier and more relaxed.'

She glanced around at them all, and then settled her gaze on James. 'I also thought we could maybe start going out more. You know, maybe have a regular date night or something? Especially now the restaurants look like they'll be opening up again.'

James nodded. 'Alright. Let's try it and see how it goes. The kids can start by clearing the table.'

Jo laughed at the groans that brought on. 'Well, how about we do it together tonight?' she suggested, standing up to help her children gather the plates.

Before the barbecue on Saturday evening, Jo told James how she felt she was being taken advantage of by his family. He had not realised how much she had been doing for his parents and said he would speak to his sisters alone.

Later that evening, James picked his moment; he waited until Jo was in the house, and then asked them why they had not been doing shopping or chores for their parents.

'Because Jo was free,' Megan said.

'And she sort of offered,' Beth added. 'Plus, Mum and Dad always ask her first!'

'Because they know Jo isn't likely to say no as much as you two do. You must realise that it's not fair. I didn't know you'd left everything for Jo to do; she's got enough on her plate at the moment looking after her own parents.'

'But I work!' Megan protested.

'So does Jo.'

'But she only works for you, doesn't she?' Beth asked.

James ignored her. 'Look, I don't want to upset you, but I'll be drawing up a rota of who is going to do what for Mum and Dad, and it will be split three ways, between you two and me. Okay? We need to make this fair, and I've been just as bad as you two have, not doing my share. We need to pick up the slack.'

The sisters glanced sideways at each other, but nodded.

With a little more free time, Jo increased the hours she spent with her parents, and started to talk to them about her current hopes and plans. Her parents, who had already noticed a new brightness about their daughter, told her that she now looked like the young Jo they remembered, the Jo who had been excited and ready to take on the world.

The following Saturday, 4th July, James took Jo out to a local pub, and they both appreciated how good it was to spend time together again. They agreed that they had both become so involved in their busy routines they had forgotten about taking care of each other. Jo was pleased when James suggested they book a weekend break at the end of September (pandemic permitting) when the kids went to university.

Jo was determined to have more quality time with both of her children before they left, so she began by taking Cassie out for a day to go clothes shopping and, as the hairdressers had now re-opened, she surprised her by booking them both in for a restyle.

Spending quality time with Jack was more of a challenge. Jo gave him lessons on how to use the washing machine and how to cook simple meals like spaghetti bolognaise. To begin with, Jack was not too happy with Jo's new expectations, but he could see that she was determined to make him capable of looking after himself and as it would be helping her out at the same time, he did as he was told.

With her family helping out more, Jo had time to set up an Instagram account to share her photos with friends and followers, and more opportunity to practice her new hobby.

Jo's crew were rallying around her, making her journey possible.

Sharon and Viv – Our Journey cont'd...

At the start of our journey, we planned to do as much as we could ourselves; we were in our boats, and it was our journey.

However, even though between us we have a wealth of knowledge, skills, and experience, we were realistic and knew that in key areas, we would need professional support. Nobody can do everything and if we wanted to do it right, we would need to look at recruiting a crew.

We produced our first list of potential crew members we would need:

- Graphic designer – for our logo, the book cover, and possibly the website
- Financial adviser/Accountant – for start-up and ongoing advice
- Solicitor – for the legal stuff
- Advance readers – to identify any obvious problems or 'typos'
- Editor – for suggestions, proofreading, and expert advice
- Publisher – to get the book out there.

As well as the professionals we needed to recruit, it was also important that we had the support of our family and friends. It was going to be a long voyage, so emotional support and an occasional kick up the backside when morale was low would be crucial.

This was not so easy. Most of our friends and family were behind us 100%. However, there were a few that needed persuading and reassuring that we had thought long and hard about the journey we were embarking on, and that we were prepared to work hard to reach our destination.

Some were also concerned that our commitment to our venture would become all-consuming at the expense of the time we spent with them.

Again, we reassured them that rowing our own boats would give us the flexibility to manage our time and to maintain our work-life balance.

We also identified that there were a few people in our lives who were not supportive, and whose attitudes had a negative impact on us.

We decided to row away from them. This was not an easy decision to make, but we knew that the challenges ahead would be hard enough without them trying to hold us back or keeping us tied to the shore.

The one area we both agreed on strongly was that while we both had family crew members who were supporting us, we had to recognise that they, in turn, might need us to support them. This could involve them having to face their own storms, including COVID-19 restrictions and limitations, ill-health, or childcare issues, and we agreed that we would do whatever was necessary to help them should the need arise.

Chapter 6 – On Course?

Row, row, row your boat,

Watch the water flow,

Rowing's fun, but rowing's hard,

This I surely know.

In this chapter we cover:

- How to assess whether you are on the right track
- Why it's okay to change course
- How to rekindle your motivation
- Appreciating your efforts so far

On every journey, it's a good idea to stop now and then and have a look at where you are. When you're making life changes, regardless of whether they are large or small, taking stock is important.

Ask yourself this question:

Am I on course?

If your answer is 'yes' and you're happy with how everything is going, you could skip this chapter (although you still may learn something useful if you read it!).

If you feel that you're doing well, please let us know (send an email to info@rowyourownboat.co.uk or a message via our Facebook page) and we may share your success story with others to inspire and motivate them.

Alternatively, you may wish to think about developing a backup plan to prepare for the unexpected and keep yourself motivated. We will look at this later in this chapter.

If your answer is 'no,' you may need to ask yourself some questions to determine what has happened and what you need to do to get back on course.

You may already know what's gone wrong and what you need to do to fix it; you just need to get on with it. Don't put off till tomorrow what you can do today. However, if there is a justifiable reason for the delay, e.g., ill health, financial problems, etc., it's okay to put things on hold for a while until you are in a position to deal with them.

Now, if you're thinking, '*But it's not my fault; something happened that has made me stop!',* we're going to cover how to deal with storms and repair your boat in Chapter 7. Again, you might still find bits of this chapter useful, but you can skip ahead if you prefer.

For many of us, working out **'Why am I not on course?'** may need a little more investigation.

Use the following table to ask and answer some questions about your journey so far. Feel free to add other questions in the blank spaces. Be honest with yourself; this is a tool to help you solve a problem and get back on course.

Ask yourself:	Your answer	What is the solution?
Where am I now?		
Am I still on the right course?		
Am I where I thought I'd be by now?		
Have I gone wrong? If so, where and why?		
Have outside influences affected my progress?		
Do I need to go back and review the choices I made?		

How am I feeling?		
Have I lost my motivation?		

If, despite answering the questions, you are still struggling, then please take a look at our Facebook page, where you may discover others who are in the same position, and we can all help each other.

For those of you who need a temporary break, now is the time to take a breather.

Drop anchor and rest for a while. Recharge your batteries and refocus your energies. Spoil yourself, catch up with friends and family, get out in the fresh air, and take some time to remind yourself why you want to *Row Your Own Boat* and the benefits this will bring to your life.

If you feel you don't need a break, let's jump straight on to how to start fixing issues.

Hopefully, you won't need to scrap everything you've done to date. Ocean liners only have to adjust their course by a couple of degrees to head in a completely different destination, and there's no reason why you can't do the same.

At the start of this chapter, you asked yourself the question *'Am I on course?'*

Do any of the following points match your response?

- I'm tired and worn out from all the effort I've been making
- I'm being pulled in so many directions, I have no time for myself
- I'm struggling on my own
- I'm bored
- It's all taking too long and I've lost my motivation
- I feel that it's all too hard
- I've lost my way

At this point, you could simply stop doing everything you've been doing, let go of your oars, and hope that you float along with the currents to your destination. However, you know that if you stop rowing towards your goal, despite everything you've done to date, you probably still won't get there. The tides may take you off in a completely different direction and you might even find yourself back where you started.

A drifting boat is one heading nowhere.

Are you letting your boat drift?

Don't let fear or self-preservation turn you away from your plan. Don't tell yourself that you'll be happy if you don't reach your goal. Don't tell yourself your goal is not worth the effort.

Look at what you've achieved by getting this far.

It may not feel like much now, but examining your life, plotting your dreams and wishes, planning your route, and setting off has already been an amazing process that will have changed you, even if it's in minor ways.

Take some time to revisit the start of your journey.

- What was your motivation?
- Has anything changed to alter this?
- Do you need to rethink and/or re-plot your course?

Return to Port?

If you look around and genuinely believe you're on the wrong course, it's one hundred percent okay to stop for a while right now.

Have a short break.

Don't work on anything for a few days.

Give yourself time to relax, to breathe easy and rest. Watch movies, play games, read books, listen to music, catch up with friends, and don't think about your plan at all. Things may not seem as bad if you come back to them with a rested body and mind.

Life will never be set in stone, so for us to live our best lives, we need to be flexible and ready to adapt and change our course.

Maybe you feel that you're still on the right course, but it just needs to be tweaked a little.

This may include changing the schedule, changing your crew, considering other suppliers or resources, or seeking specialist advice to reach your destination.

Revising the plan may be the boost you need to pick up your oars and start rowing again, putting you back in charge of your own boat.

If you decide 100% that you're on the wrong route, you can always go right back to Chapter 1 and go through the 'Where am I now?' questions, and then follow them up with 'Where do I want to go?' and 'How am I going to get there?'

Nothing is stopping you from making a whole new plan. If that's what you decide you need to do, that's fine.

Don't be afraid to plot a new course.

You may like the new destination better!

This is YOUR boat and YOUR journey, and only YOU can decide on your destination.

No matter how far you've gone along your charted route, if it's not what you expected or you've come to realise that you're going in the wrong direction, you are free to do whatever you need to do to put it right.

Many things in life turn out to be not quite what we expected or hoped for, including our education, relationships, new job roles, training courses, new hobbies, and so on.

We've all set off on journeys full of enthusiasm and optimism, only to be disappointed by the truth once we're underway, or even when we have the destination in sight.

Everything you do in life gives you valuable lessons and insights, so ask yourself the following questions:

- What have I learned from this journey?
- What can I do better the next time I set off?
- Can I identify any extra steps that I should have taken?
- Have I wasted time doing things I didn't need to do?
- Was I influenced by others, instead of being true to myself?
- Should I have asked for or accepted help from others?
- Did I let my fear of admitting a mistake overshadow the need to start again?

If asking these questions has not helped you to get back in your boat and start rowing again, imagine this:

Someone close to you has been rowing towards their dream destination and they are beginning to struggle. Life keeps putting obstacles in their way and even though they've managed to navigate their way around them, they're running out of steam.

You've noticed that they are having difficulties and want to help. You know how important their target is to them and that they don't want to give up.

What would you say to encourage them to pick up their oars and start rowing again? How would you respond if they said they wanted to return to shore and plan another route?

Imagine the conversation you would have with them.

Now have that conversation with yourself.

GETTING BACK ON COURSE

If you think you're on the right course but you're just '*not feeling it*,' let's try and relight that spark of motivation. After all the work you've done, it's worth trying a few tricks to see if you can rediscover your mojo.

Here are a few simple things you can try:

- Write notes to yourself to remind you of your goals. Put them where you can see them, as a screensaver on your PC or laptop, on your bedside table, on your planner or calendar, in your wallet, or even on your fridge.
- Find or draw pictures to illustrate your goals and add them to your notes.
- Revise your target dates and adjust your motivational rewards or treats.
- Visualise yourself in the future when you've arrived at your destination or achieved your goal.
- Find and play music that makes you feel good.
- Sign up for a course to improve the skills you may need to reach your goal.
- Search for motivational quotes and find a few that ring true to you. Write them down and keep them close.
- Find a companion in another boat and row alongside them.
- Join a support group to find like-minded rowers.

Many people give up because they look at how far they've still got to go, instead of looking at how far they've come.

Glance back at where you were when you started this whole process and compare it to where you are now.

A short while ago, you were probably only dreaming of where you are now, so use this to put your achievements into perspective!

Even if you've lost your way right now, things will work out if you decide they will and if you trust your plan.

> *"Just because you failed once doesn't mean you are going to fail at everything."*
>
> *Marilyn Monroe*

It's okay to have a break now and then to stop, look around, and appreciate how far you've come, but as soon as you feel refreshed, get back at the oars and start rowing again.

If others are doubting your abilities, let them.

If anyone has been criticising or mocking you, ignore them.

Stay strong and be true to yourself and your plan.

Decide you will be someone who succeeds.

Visualise yourself and the feeling of happiness and pride you will experience when you've reached your destination and achieved your personal goal.

Can you bounce back?

Are you resilient?

The dictionary definition of resilience is that a person is able to withstand or recover quickly from difficult conditions.

Resilience isn't about continuing your journey regardless of how you feel; it's about your ability to bounce back when something knocks you down.

Resilience can grow and change during your life, depending on your experiences.

You may have had many times when you felt that you couldn't cope, that you could not carry on, but if you look back now, you've always got through them.

Everyone handles stress differently; some people seem to cope with everything life throws at them, while others can find small setbacks overwhelming.

Some people appear to sail through life effortlessly, no matter what befalls them. These people have probably developed simple techniques which have helped them to face and deal with these situations.

Here are a few ideas you can try to build resilience:

- Look at your difficulties as temporary challenges, not permanent factors.
- Examine your response to every situation carefully. Is it appropriate? What would you do differently next time? Are you influenced by what you think others expect of you?
- Rise above the temptation to play the victim. Focus on changing the things you CAN control and not those you CAN'T.
- Think back to all the bad things you've already got through, draw strength from the way you dealt with them, and reassure yourself that you can handle difficult situations.
- Remember that positive thinking can help you to get through the doldrums.
- Look forward to your brightest future.
- Whenever possible, try to see the funny side of the situation.
- Look after your physical health.
- Always make time to have fun.

Another useful tool to help to keep yourself motivated and to restore your self-esteem is the use of personal affirmations. These are simple statements you can say out loud to reinforce your true worth.

To many of us, this may sound daft, and the thought of saying positive things about ourselves is so far outside our comfort zones, it makes us cringe. However, give it a go, you might find it's not as bad as you expect!

You may find it helpful to build a personal list of affirmations you can use, but here are a few to start you off:

- I am rowing my own boat.
- I am making an impact on the world.

- I am kind.
- I am good.
- I am smart.
- I am capable.
- I am honest.
- I am loyal.
- I am loving.
- I am caring.
- I trust my decisions and will follow them through.
- I am confident that I can create the life I want.
- **I am me!**

Add your own statements to this list and repeat at least one, if not all of them, every day, as many times as you need to. Remind yourself how amazing you are!

None of your goals and aspirations have been carved in stone; you can scrap, amend, or follow them to the letter. It's up to you and you alone.

If you start to follow a Plan B, remember that you can always change your mind again later and go back to Plan A.

There are 26 letters in the English alphabet, and you can use them all if you need to!

Over the next few weeks, Sam sounded out his contacts. Most were keen to work with him, but the pandemic had hit local businesses hard; many were struggling to stay afloat, and some had gone under.

It was not a good time to start an events business, either. All large events had been completely banned, and only small numbers of people were allowed to attend weddings and funerals. Therefore, although Sam knew he had all the skills, experience, and ambition to be successful, this was not the right time.

Sam went back to his notes and looked at his original mind map. He decided to change tack and scale down his plans to fit in with the new guidelines. It also occurred to him that doing so would allow him to build his reputation, develop a client base, and establish a team of suppliers he could depend on.

He looked at his 'party in a box' idea and decided to offer the boxes to single households or support bubbles. His idea was simple: he would supply afternoon teas or boxes of party supplies to people's homes.

This would still enable Sam to use his skills and expertise, offering a quality service that would bring people a few hours of joy, despite the chaos of the world.

Afternoon tea in a box had been on his original plan, but parties in a box hadn't, so he did need to slightly alter his course. Despite that, he liked both ideas, and he felt they were achievable in the current climate.

Sam updated his action plan:

- *Contact known (trusted) local suppliers*
- *Research competitors (service provided and costings)*
- *Research suppliers for items not available locally*
- *Marketing – flyers, leaflets, posters*
- *Website*
- *Online parties*
- *Legal requirements – GDPR, etc.*
- *COVID-19 compliance*
- *Finance*

Sam then rewrote his mind map:

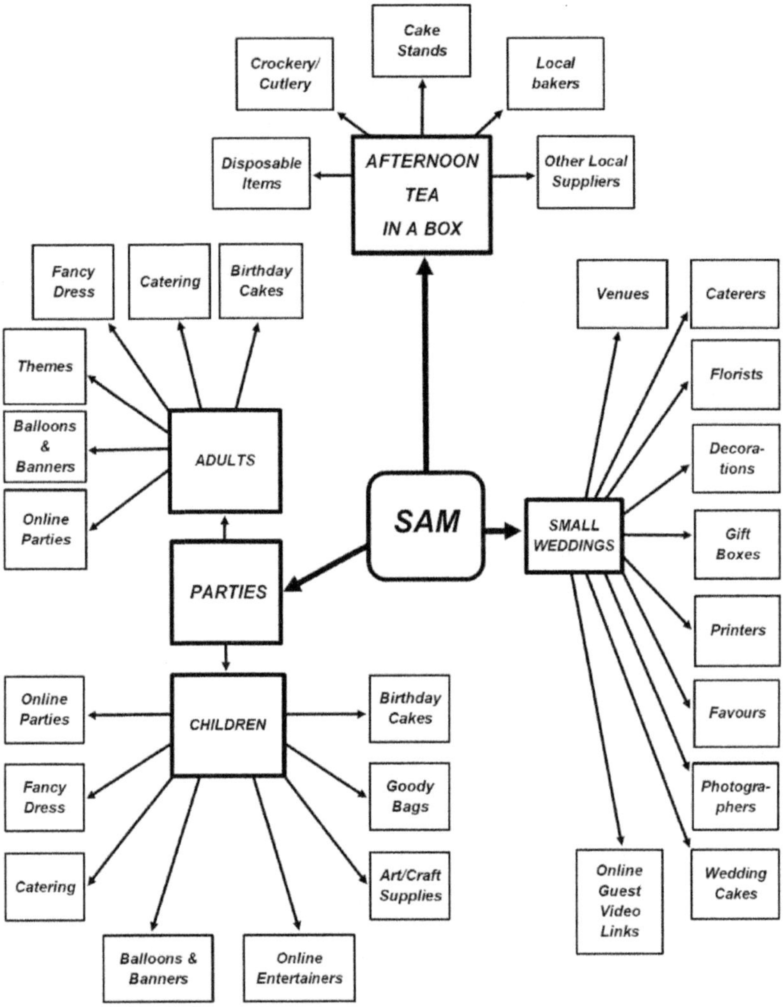

Sam thought about his new business and realised that giving his custom to local companies at this difficult time might also help them to diversify and ultimately stay afloat. It would be a win-win scenario.

As the summer progressed, Jack began to take an interest in Jo's photography. He was very impressed when she showed him some of the pictures she had taken.

'These are amazing, mum,' he said. 'You should have a go at doing something with them.'

'Like what?'

'I don't know... there are loads of websites where you can get pictures put on mugs or make calendars.'

'I don't know how to do any of that.'

Jack grinned. 'I'll help you. I don't think it's hard.'

'I'd like to do something for Sam. He's helped me so much this year, and I'm really proud of the progress he's made.'

'Come on,' Jack said. 'Let's have a look now.'

An hour later, Jack had helped Jo to produce and order a calendar full of pictures of Bobby, and a mug for him with a really cute photo of Bobby on it. Jo thought Sam could give the calendar to Bobby's owners and keep the mug for himself.

When the calendar arrived a few days later, Jo was so pleased with the results that she called the shelter and made an appointment to take some photos of their animals and show them some of her images along with Bobby's calendar.

The meeting went well. The shelter manager loved her photographs of Bobby and their rescue animals. Although one of their staff had tried to prepare a calendar for 2021, they said it was not as good as the one Jo had produced. The charity was struggling, and a possible second wave of COVID-19 looming on the horizon meant that their situation looked set to get even worse, so any help was welcome.

Jo agreed to put together a formal proposal, with a mock-up of how their calendar would look, by the end of the week.

That evening, James was surprised to find their dining room had been converted into a work room. Jo was surrounded by printouts of the shelter animals, and a few price lists which Jack had researched for her.

She had also spoken to Sam, who had given her the contact details of a local print shop he knew. The print shop had even offered a charity discount for them.

Two weeks later, Jo's proposal to the animal shelter was given the go-ahead. Now, more than ever, the charity needed the financial income the calendars would raise, and the pressure was on Jo to make them the best they could be. She worked hard, utilising Jack's IT skills and James's attention to detail to get the final draft finished. After a few minor tweaks, the shelter manager approved it and the calendar went to print.

The sight of her calendar on the shelter's website and social media pages, helping to promote the charity and raise much-needed funds, brought Jo closer to her goals; she now felt she was giving something back and making a difference.

Jo was still enjoying her family time, especially now the chores were better distributed.

Towards the end of the month, she visited Sam to deliver his gifts. He was delighted with his mug and loved the calendar so much that he asked if she could order another one for him to keep. She was flattered that he was so impressed with her work and ordered the calendar that evening.

Weekly date nights with James were also going well, and James had booked a weekend away for them at the beginning of October.

Jo began to feel happier than she had for a long time and, despite the pandemic, she was optimistic about the future.

Sharon and Viv – Our Journey cont'd...

As the weeks passed, we continued at our day jobs and used our spare time to work on the book. For a few months, we were able to get together on Saturdays, when we reviewed our progress and planned what the next stage would be.

During the week, we would catch up via phone calls, emails, and video chats. Given everything that was against us, we were pleased with our progress. We still had a lot to do, but we were making headway.

In the autumn, the UK government introduced tiered restrictions due to the rise in the number of COVID-19 cases. Our face-to-face Saturday meetings had to be shelved and, as we both worked best when we could bounce ideas off each other in person, our progress suffered.

We were both working longer hours and although we kept in regular contact, we realised that we needed to stop, drop anchor, and assess our journey.

We asked ourselves these questions:

- Where are we now?
- Are we where we thought we would be?
- Are we still on the right course?

Our progress had slowed down a knot or two and although we were not where we had hoped to be, we had come a long way, and we both agreed that we were still on the right course.

Our desire to continue rowing our own boats was as strong as ever, and we felt that as long as we could keep rowing towards our destination, albeit at a slower pace, we would get there. Over Christmas we both took a short break to recharge, and then plunged back into the book with renewed energy.

We kept each other motivated, chatted via video calls, and updated/edited each other's files electronically. It was difficult, but we managed.

We agreed that 2021 was going to be **our year** and that we wanted to be ready to help our fellow rowers as life began to return to normal, whatever that would look like.

We both picked up the oars and started rowing with a renewed sense of purpose. We still had to communicate via email, video calls, and the telephone, but we felt optimistic and hopeful for the future.

We accepted that our timeframes for the book and related work might have to be altered, but that was okay. The important thing was to keep rowing.

> *Perseverance is the key.*
>
> *Believe in what you are doing and keep going.*

To help keep ourselves motivated and our spirits high, we used affirmations we would quote to each other. These included:

We ARE smart.

We CAN do this.

We ARE capable.

We WILL make a difference.

We ARE rowing our own boats!

This is our journey, our plan, our dreams, our wishes, and our destination – and it goes way beyond the bounds of this one book!

Chapter 7 – Storms of life

Row, row, row your boat,

Gently to the beach,

If you see a school of sharks,

You are allowed to screech!

In this chapter we cover:

- What storms are and how to assess your stress levels
- Techniques that will help you handle them

Feeling all at sea?

We may all go through storms on our voyages. Unfortunately, some storms are more like raging tempests that hurl us from one overwhelming wave to another with no let-up.

One storm can be hard enough to cope with, but life, being life, often throws more than one storm at us at a time and this can send us spiralling into despair, and sometimes make us question whether we will even survive.

Are you in the middle of a storm?

Is your boat being tossed around by rough seas and massive waves?

Are you scared you may capsize?

Do you feel like you're sinking, or even that you could fall overboard and drown under the weight of events that are going on in your life?

There are things you can do to weather the storm, but first, you should simply stop and take a good look at the storm that you are going through.

Ask yourself if it's just a passing squall. If so, if you hold your nerve and hang on, will it pass by itself?

If not, then this chapter is for you.

Few of us are completely stormproof, and nor can we turn our boats into submarines, dive to the depths, and wait out the storm.

The majority of us, as we row our boats, will encounter bad weather. The good news is that most of us manage to survive whatever the storms throw at us and come out the other side stronger.

You will know when a storm hits and, depending on the circumstances, you will probably try to cope with it in tried-and-tested ways. However, before you can work out how to handle your storm, you need to identify what kind of storm it is.

Can you pinpoint why this storm has come into your life? Is it a random event, something that no one could have foreseen, or has it been brought about by the actions of someone else – or maybe even yourself?

If the storm has come about because of something you did, can you put it right? If you can, do so quickly.

If someone else is responsible, there are many things you could try:

- Take a detour to avoid it.
- Talk to the person or people concerned and explain how their actions are affecting you. Ask them to stop, or at least to calm things down.
- Learn new coping mechanisms (you'll find a few hints and tips about these later in this chapter).

Dealing with big life events

The storms of life come in many forms, but the one thing they all have in common is change and the stress this brings.

Every major life event – whether a birth, a death, ill health, marriage, separation, employment, housing issues, or something else – brings its own set of problems and changes we must cope with.

Even happy events can feel like a typhoon has hit. Every birth, no matter how welcome, brings massive changes to a family. This can be as much a storm as the death of a loved one. A wedding or big celebration can become an all-consuming event, which will be the focus of every conversation and almost every thought until it is over.

You are affected by every tiny squall or massive storm your boat goes through, and they can all add up.

The stress of these events can cause both mental and physical problems.

The Holmes and Rahe Stress Scale

In 1967, psychiatrists Thomas Holmes and Richard Rahe surveyed over 5,000 medical patients and asked them if they had experienced any of a series of 43 life events (Life Change Units) in the previous two years.

They gave each event a different 'weight' score for stress.

They measured how many stressful events patients had experienced, and how 'weighted' these events were and used these to create a total score. The higher this score was, the more likely the patient was to become ill. Although this scale was developed in America over 50 years ago, it applies just the same today, no matter where you live.

How to rate your current stress levels

You'll find the Holmes and Rahe Stress Scale on the next page.

To complete it, if you've experienced any of the events listed in the last 12 to 18 months, or you are expecting any in the near future, write the 'Impact Score' into the 'My Score' column, and then add up your score at the bottom.

If any of the events have happened more than once, multiply your score accordingly.

Your results will show the likelihood of you soon becoming physically ill (if you're not already suffering).

If you scored	Your likelihood of illness is:
300+	about 80 percent
150 - 299	about 50 percent
Less than 150	about 30 percent

The higher your life change score, the more care you will need to take to get yourself back into a state of good health.

Life Change Index Scale (The Stress Test)		
Event	**Impact Score**	**My Score**
Death of spouse	100	
Divorce	73	
Marital separation	65	
Jail term	63	
Death of a close family member	63	
Personal injury or illness	53	
Marriage	50	
Fired at work	47	
Marital reconciliation	45	
Retirement	45	
Change in health of family member	44	
Pregnancy	40	
Sex difficulties	39	
Gain of a new family member	39	
Business readjustment	39	
Change in financial state	38	
Death of a close friend	37	
Change to a different line of work	36	
Change in number of arguments with spouse	35	
Mortgage over $150,000 (*Updated in 2018*)	31	
Foreclosure of mortgage or loan	30	
Change in responsibilities at work	29	
Son or daughter leaving home	29	
Trouble with in-laws	29	
Outstanding personal achievement	28	
Spouse begins or stops work	26	
Children begin or end school	26	
Change in living conditions	25	
Revisions of personal habits	24	
Trouble with boss	23	
Change in work hours or conditions	20	
Change in residence	20	
Change in schools	20	
Change in recreations	19	
Change in church activities	19	
Change in social activities	19	
Mortgage/loan less than $150,000 (*Updated in 2018*)	17	
Change in sleeping habits	16	
Change in number of family get-togethers	15	
Change in eating habits	15	
Vacation	13	
Christmas approaching	12	
Minor violation of the law	11	
	Total	

After completing this scale, you now know what the most stressful life events are and what you are coping with, but as you pass through these storms, what can you expect and how can you deal with them?

There is no *'one size fits all'* method for coping with major life events. What helps one person to get through something may not be right for another.

If you're going through one (or more) of these life storms, don't feel bad if you think you're not getting through it as well or as fast as you (or others) think you should.

Before looking at how to cope, let's ask the question; what is the common factor in all our storms?

CHANGE

Everyone handles change differently. This is your journey, your individual situation, and these are your emotions. Take as much time as you need to weather your storm.

We all have to deal with changes in our lives. These periods of transition are hard to go through but if you manage them poorly, you can make things worse.

We all need to work through our emotions and reactions to change.

If a loved one passes away or a close relationship ends and you do not use the support which is available, it may prolong the period you need to heal and recover.

If you lose your job but allow it to affect you so badly that you sit at home suffering from despair and depression, you will be unable (mentally and physically) to apply for other work.

You can always make a bad storm worse by resisting or not accepting the changes which come with it, but if you handle it well, a storm can often work in your favour in the long run.

Major life events and changes are some of the most difficult storms to get through, but at the end of each tempest, you will often find an opportunity to improve things or to grow as a person.

Unfortunately, when you're being belted by lashing rain, when you're being tossed around by rough seas and hanging on for dear life, you may not be able to see that far ahead.

Ways to cope with changes

If you know a storm is coming, you can try to protect yourself from some of the effects in the following ways:

- Learn as much about your storm as possible. The fear of the unknown is often much worse than the actual experience.

- If your changes are self-made, limit how many changes you make in any given period. It can take time to adjust to change, so be patient before tackling another.

- Discuss any problems you think you're likely to have handling your storm with someone who can help (family, friends, or professionals).

Because any change can cause stress, you might become anxious or depressed. You may feel more tired than usual but have trouble sleeping. Many people experience headaches or find that they don't eat as they would normally (either too much or too little). Some turn to drugs or alcohol or other dangerous behaviours.

Before things get out of hand, you might be able to help yourself a little first. When you see a big storm approaching, there's a little exercise you can do to change the way you look at it.

Think of the event you are currently experiencing or are about to experience and ask yourself the following questions:

What has or is **ACTUALLY** going to change?

What has or will **ACTUALLY** be staying the same?

Think about how you might be affected. If you can prepare yourself for it, you may be able to take some of the pressure off before you enter the heart of the storm.

Think about what the storm (event) will involve:

Will your usual environments change?

- Your home?
- Your workplace?
- Will you still have loved ones or other important people close?

Will you have to change your routines?

Do you believe you can cope with the change? If not, why not?

Do you need to improve your knowledge or skills?

If you find yourself struggling with your reactions to the storm and feel that your emotions are getting out of control, stop, take a deep breath, and try to do something about it.

If you start to feel overwhelmed, write down exactly how you're feeling, and the options you have for working through it. If you can't see that far ahead, it's time to make a few adjustments.

EMERGENCY REPAIRS

If you can see that things may get messy or if you feel out of control, what can you do to help yourself in the short term?

You can make a few emergency repairs yourself, like patching holes or waterproofing your boat to make yourself feel better. You could start with the following actions:

Friends and family

The people closest to you can be really helpful, either by listening or by providing practical support.

Could any of them allow you to tie your boat to theirs for a while? Maybe they would let you ride in their boat and give you time to rest while they row you through the worst of it?

If anyone you know has been through a similar storm, talk to them first; they will probably have the benefit of hindsight and may be able to offer you sensible insights which might help.

Make and follow a routine

If your storm brings a whole new way of living and you feel disorientated, start by making a new routine to give yourself a sense of control over at least some parts of your life.

Plan and follow a good early morning routine. Get up at the same time and have breakfast. Go for a run/walk, meditate, listen to music – do anything which will help you to relax enough that you can face the day feeling in control.

Relaxation Techniques

To help you to lower your stress levels:

- Have a long soak in a hot bath
- Listen to music or sing along to your favourite songs
- Learn and practise a new relaxation technique
- Light candles or burn aromatherapy oils
- Treat yourself to a massage

Do anything that you think will help you to relax, but avoid turning to drugs, alcohol, or other addictive behaviours, (you know these will make things worse in the long run.)

Laugh

Although you may not feel like it, plan to have fun, schedule time in your diary to enjoy yourself or meet friends for a meal and a catch-up. Watch a hilarious movie or TV series, or go to the park and get on a swing and enjoy the freedom. Laughing (even if you don't feel like it) can make you feel better, reduce your stress levels, and leave you feeling more positive.

Exercise

You don't need to join a gym and wear yourself out. Any exercise is good for you, so try to move your body every day. Go for a walk, turn on the radio, play bouncy music and dance around your home, or go for a swim at the local pool. Anything that makes you a little breathless will leave you feeling brighter for a while.

Nutrition

Your basic bodily needs should not be ignored, so even though you may not want to pay attention to your diet when you are feeling low, you should.

If you can, plan a few meals in advance, write a list, go shopping for the ingredients, and then concentrate on cooking good, nutritious meals.

As you prepare the food, pay attention to the acts of chopping and stirring. Enjoy the colours and aromas and then savour every mouthful.

Even if you've lost your appetite, remind yourself that you can't row your own boat if you don't give your body the fuel it needs to function.

Grow your social network

If you can, try not to restrict yourself to social media. Go out and find people to join forces with.

- Sign up for a class
- Volunteer for a charity
- Visit your local social club
- Look at local groups for people with similar interests or hobbies
- Reach out to family and friends you have not contacted for a while

When you're grieving or feeling stressed, these activities may feel as daunting as deciding to climb a mountain. However, you must bear in mind that any of these can help you to build a network of people you can call on, so it's worth the effort.

If you find that your social media accounts are making you feel worse, have a break for a while, or block people who drag you down.

Go outside

Leave your home at least once every day, even if you only walk around the block or to the local shop. If you can, try to visit a green space (your local recreation ground or park is fine) where you can stroll, listen to the birds, and observe nature.

It's easy to become a recluse when you feel anxious and to convince yourself that staying at home is the safest thing to do. Instead, visit family or meet up with friends as often as you can.

Change your work-life balance

Where possible, allow yourself more time off. Working yourself into a frenzy for a job is never a good idea. Even if you are self-employed, you must take a reasonable amount of time off to relax.

Offload heavy cargo

At work or home, if you realise you're responsible for too many things, delegate some of them. If the load you're hauling becomes too heavy, the weight of it could sink your boat; so you need to steer clear of that.

Waterlogged but not scuppered

When you feel as though everything around you has gone wrong, that you've got nothing left to fall back on or that your future is bleak, you need to stop and take a bearing.

At this point, you should remind yourself that nothing in life is permanent.

The storms you are going through will pass. The raging seas you are trying to navigate will soon be calm, and the turbulent waves will eventually become ripples.

You may not be able to see it right now, but in time, everything you are going through will be a memory.

WHEN TO SEEK PROFESSIONAL HELP

The expression *'Fake it till you make it'* is often used by well-meaning people, but it's not good advice.

You may sometimes have to deal with storms alone, but never be afraid to reach out to others if you can. Some signs that you may need input from loved ones or professionals include when you realise that:

- You can no longer pretend that you feel okay
- You find it difficult to enjoy your usual hobbies or activities
- You are unable to follow your usual routines
- You avoid family or friends
- You experience a change in your sleeping patterns
- You've changed your eating habits
- You feel anxious or depressed
- You are overwhelmed by panic or stress
- You engage in dangerous behaviour(s)
- You feel suicidal

GET HELP!

We all have our bad days, but if they persist and your feelings and mood don't improve, don't just hope it will pass.

If you feel that you're sinking, that you're going underwater and drowning, send out an SOS for help.

Seek medical and/or emotional help as soon as it occurs to you that you need it.

Don't just hang on and hope for the best.

Don't *'put on a brave face'* and try to get through your bad times alone.

THERAPY

You may find that it helps to talk about your life changes and how you're coping with them (or not) with a therapist, so contact your medical practitioner/GP as soon as you begin to feel overwhelmed.

Many people wait until they can't take any more, when they've fallen overboard and are in danger of drowning. At that stage, they may find it much harder to get back into their boat, so don't wait until you hit a crisis point.

There are many kinds of therapy available to help you to cope with the storms you've been through or those you are currently experiencing. You may also find help by joining support groups, or by contacting your local medical centre for advice.

If you feel suicidal, even for a moment, talk to your GP, who can direct you to the right port for the storm you are going through.

If you can't speak to your GP, contact the Samaritans:

Call (free)	116 123 or
Email	jo@samaritans.org
Website	https://www.samaritans.org

When life is hard and you are struggling with something, you may either try to avoid the storm or detour around it, although you know deep down inside that ignoring something doesn't usually make it go away.

If there's no other option you will have to face your storms head-on and row through them. If you don't take in the sails and batten down the hatches, but choose to row through a maelstrom unprepared, you're much more likely to suffer damage.

It won't be obvious, but most people you meet have faced their own storms. They may have known chaos, felt all alone, lost at sea and tossed around, but they have battled their way through their storms and have come out the other side.

These people may be able to offer support and they could provide a wealth of advice and guidance, as they will appreciate how difficult life is for you right now.

If you don't know anyone in your life who has gone through similar storms to the ones you are facing, search for counselling services on the internet.

Every individual has to row through unsettled weather – calm one day, tempestuous the next – but most of us get through our storms eventually.

Look back at how many storms you've already survived; it may not have been easy, but you've weathered hurricanes and typhoons, tropical storms and blizzards, and every single one has helped to make you the person you are today.

Every trial you've been through has made you stronger.

Every painful incident on your journey can make you more appreciative of the good things when you find them.

With courage and determination,

you can and you will get through this.

In October, with COVID-19 cases in the UK rising steeply, the government introduced a three-tier system to combat the pandemic. Sam's area was put into Level 2, so the hotel remained open. Despite the fact that he was working, Sam chose to press on with his plans for running his own business.

He made contact with local suppliers, and many were keen to work with him. He also started taking online courses to upgrade his IT skills, and began looking into building a website.

As his birthday approached, Sam decided to celebrate virtually. He put together party boxes for each of the households he had invited, containing a variety of party snacks and drinks. He added party hats and streamers, together with a personal message from him. He then delivered them all with strict instructions that they should not be opened until they were all together on a group video call. The party was a huge success.

Following the party, Sam was asked if he could provide similar boxes for other special occasions, tailoring them to suit the event and the budget. He soon realised that the possibilities were endless and that his boxes could be sent anywhere across the country.

He felt optimistic about the future, but there were storm clouds on the horizon.

One morning, Sam received a call from Bobby's elderly owner, Pat, letting him know that her husband, John, had been rushed into hospital with breathing problems and had tested positive for COVID-19. Pat could not be with John and had to isolate until her test results came back.

Sam offered to help in any way he could, but Pat said that he would also need to isolate and take a test, as a few days ago, Sam had helped John to carry shopping into their house.

Sam had not realised that such a simple act of kindness could put his life at risk. He also realised that, as he was in a support bubble with his mum, she could be at risk too. He called to tell her and reassured her that he felt fine but had to isolate until his test result came back.

He then contacted the hotel. The manager was understanding and told Sam to let him know the result of his test as soon as he got it. He reassured him that he had probably not put anyone else at risk as all the staff had been practising social distancing and wore masks at work.

Sam's fears for his mum, colleagues, friends, and his own health were very real, but everyone seemed understanding and keen to reassure him – except for one colleague.

The man in question was furious with Sam for putting them at risk. Sam's explanation about his neighbour needing help fell on deaf ears, and he soon found himself blocked on Facebook with a nasty message about taking responsibility. It stung, but Sam knew he'd done the right thing, and all he could do now was isolate.

He made provisional arrangements, in case his test was positive, for a friend to take over doing his mum's shopping and bring him food too, and then settled down to wait.

The following twenty-four hours were very stressful, especially when he thought about his mother. He had acted with the best of intentions, but even so, he had put her at risk.

When the negative test result arrived, Sam's relief nearly knocked him off his feet. He called his mother, a few friends, and his manager, and then he called Pat. Thankfully, although she had tested positive, her symptoms were not as severe as John's, and her last call from the hospital had told her that John was improving.

Relieved, Sam promised to keep in touch with her daily and drop shopping off for her. When Pat's next test came up negative, Sam took over walking Bobby twice per day. He enjoyed the extra exercise and it gave him more time to think about his recent scare, as well as his new business, his job, and how he could keep making his life better.

Jack started university in September, followed by Cassie's return a week later. With COVID-19 on the rise again, Jo was concerned about them both, but she hoped they would be sensible and take care of themselves.

Their booked weekend away had to be postponed, but James and Jo took the time to share long walks and leisurely meals at home together and simply appreciated each other's company. Jo was enjoying herself, and although she still had not decided which way to take her photography in the long-term, she had started an online course, which she was loving. She visited the shelter regularly, taking pictures of their new animals, and felt a wash of satisfaction whenever a photo went live on their site or social media. It wasn't a grand contribution to solving the problems of the world, but it was something she could give to others, and that was all that mattered.

She missed her children considerably at times; Jack was under Tier 3 restrictions, and while he was safe, well, and enjoying the university experience, Jo found it strange not having him at home. He called a couple of times a week, as did Cassie – until a Tuesday in early November, when Jo picked up the landline to a stranger's voice, and found out that her daughter had been hospitalised following a serious car crash.

It was a storm like no other. Jo and James had no warning, no preparation time, and no action that they could take. With high COVID-19 restrictions and limited information besides the fact that Cassie's leg was broken and the hospital was conducting further tests, all they could do was wait.

A couple of nerve-wracking hours later, a doctor notified them that Cassie had a broken femur, some bruising on her upper body from the seatbelt but there were no other serious injuries. They were waiting for an orthopaedic surgeon to look at the scans to decide what the best treatment would be and that he would call them again after the surgeon had made his decision.

It was after midnight when they received another call telling them that Cassie would be operated on first thing in the morning, and that they would be putting a metal plate on the bone which would be secured with screws to hold it into place. James asked if there would be any long-term effects and the reply was that this injury could have damaged the muscles, tendons, ligaments, and nerves of the leg, but they would not be able to diagnose that until after the operation.

Jo and James had very little sleep that night. James cuddled Jo and reassured her that as Cassie was young and strong that she would be fine in a couple of months, and they both knew that she would be well cared for, but like most mothers, Jo was extremely concerned.

Cassie was taken to surgery at 8am and Jo spent the next few hours aimlessly wandering around the house, unable to concentrate on anything, worrying about her beloved daughter and what the outcome would be. At noon they had a call to say that the operation had gone well and that Cassie was in the recovery room. They were advised to call back after 6pm and that by then they might be able to talk to her.

Jo and James had decided not to tell Jack straight away, especially as under Tier 3 rules he would not be able to leave his area and they knew he would want to come home. Now that they knew Cassie was going to be alright, they let him know what had happened, told him there was nothing he could do to help, and promised to keep him informed.

Again, the hours dragged for Jo until James called the hospital and was told that Cassie was sitting up in bed, she had had her evening meal and that the police had just delivered her handbag which had her mobile phone in it, so they could call her on that.

James made a video call to their daughter and Jo was reassured to see that apart from being on a drip for pain medication, Cassie looked pale and tired but okay. Luckily, she did not remember much about the accident, but had been told that she would be up on crutches the next day and that, if everything went well, she might be sent home in around a week.

After the call Jo found herself sobbing with relief. She felt as though she had been holding her breath for hours, almost drowning under a sea of fear of what could have happened to her precious girl. Being unable to rush to her daughter's side and not knowing what the outcome of the operation would be had been both guilt inducing and terrifying in equal measure.

Eight days later, when Cassie was released from hospital (walking with crutches), Jo was relieved to see her arrive home looking well. Luckily there had been no complications or long-lasting effects, so Cassie was looking forward to returning to a normal lifestyle as soon as she could. Jo set about making her comfortable, happy at last that she could finally look after her daughter.

As the whole country was once again under lockdown, Jo was unable to visit the animal shelter, so she spent most of her time caring for Cassie and continued with her online photography course.

As December approached, Jo began to feel more at ease. Yes, it had been a hard time, but Cassie was recovering well and things had settled down nicely.

Sharon and Viv – Our Journey cont'd...

Since we stepped into our boats, picked up our oars, and started to row, we've had to face the storms of life, both on an individual basis and during our *Row Your Own Boat* journey.

Individually, we both had health issues.

Viv – I have had a back/leg problem which was diagnosed as Piriformis Syndrome and sciatica. This was extremely painful and for 6 weeks I did not leave the house, except for physio sessions. Although I was able to work on the book, I was unable to do anything else, which was very frustrating.

Sharon – After months of telephone consultations with my GP and several courses of antibiotics, an infection in my cheek still would not heal. The lump continued to grow and moved further down to my jawline and then started to weep through the skin. I sent photographs to my GP but nothing was done due to COVID-19. Eventually, I insisted on seeing a GP in person. Swabs of the site were taken but came back inconclusive. Then the storm hit; I was referred for a biopsy for cancer. This was a major concern as there is a history of cancer in my family. My boat was battered heavily by the storm and focusing on any project became hard – but I stuck it out and continued working, whilst waiting for the results of the test.

The nationwide lockdown restrictions also had a real impact on us both. Not being able to work face-to-face continued to have a major impact on our progress. We both began to feel our destination was drifting further and further away from us. We needed to jolly each other along and bounce ideas around together, in person, and this wasn't the same over a video call or on the telephone, so it hit us hard.

We were both still finding work demanding, too. There were extra hours to be done, in jobs that were already physically and mentally demanding. On top of that, we had to ensure we kept ourselves and our loved ones safe. It was hard giving 100% to our jobs and to *Row Your Own Boat*. We've always been committed to doing and being the best we can, but we were concerned that we wouldn't reach our destination if we continued working at this pace.

At the same time as trying to manage our work commitments, we also found ourselves providing extra help and support to our families as the lockdown restrictions rocked their boats. We've always agreed that our families come first, and we couldn't let them down when they needed us.

Balancing all these pressures and demands left us feeling battered by the waves the storms were throwing at us and, to be honest, we did wonder if our boats would survive.

We had many emotional conversations, early in the morning or late at night, as we were both stressed and anxious about the future. Many tears were shed, and when we each needed hugs from our best friend, it simply wasn't allowed.

We had no choice but to hang on, work as well as we could and wait the storm out.

Chapter 8 – After the Storm

Row, row, row your boat,

Now the sea is calm,

Having a break; a little rest

Won't do you any harm!

In this chapter we cover:

- Resting after a storm
- Recognising the value of storms
- Preparing for future storms

When the worst of your storm is over, when the clouds have passed, your sea will, in time, become calm again.

When you feel up to it, look back and see if you can identify how and why the storm came about, and what it taught you as you went through it (about yourself, your boat, your crew, or your planned course).

To begin with, this might feel impossible, especially if your storm was traumatic, so the best thing to do in the first instance is often to simply stop and take a breather. Drop your anchor, hold back on all actions, and allow yourself time to rest and recover and take stock of where you are now and what state your boat's in.

Your dream destination won't be going anywhere without you, so you can stop for a break without destroying your plans. If the storm has been monumental, you might now doubt whether your dream is even your dream anymore, and that's okay.

Stop and take stock.

Assess your boat now that the storm has passed. If you are ready to carry on, do so. However, you may feel battered and bruised, and this could take a while to get over, so there's no need to rush back into old habits or try to pretend nothing has happened. Just relax for a while and give yourself the time you need to decide what you want to do next.

You are not in a race!

You may be mourning a loss (people, pets, jobs, health, etc.), so be patient with yourself as you go through waves of emotional reactions to your new situation. Think of this time as a period of adjustment, a pause where you can learn to adapt to any new circumstances you find yourself in.

The nature of a storm and its impact will be different for everyone and there's no single way to deal with the aftermath. You have to find your own way through, reaching out to others when you need to.

Did the storm come about as a result of something you did (or didn't) do? Identifying the cause may help you to ensure that you avoid it in the future. However, it's important not to try and avoid all storms; many are just part of life, and we have to deal with them the best we can.

Whether you caused the storm or not, is there anything you can do to put things right for everyone involved? If so, do it immediately.

If you made a mistake and your storm dragged other people into it, apologise to them. If you can, build bridges with anyone who was harmed by it. If possible, reassure them that it won't happen again.

Everyone makes mistakes now and then. Some of these can be put right, while others can't. Whichever category yours falls under, make sure you learn from the experience, so you don't repeat it.

As you reflect on what has happened, you may need time to reassess everyone in your crew and the parts they played during the storm.

You might realise that some of your crew (maybe the people you least expected) stepped up and helped to get you through it. Some may have put their lives on hold to stop and throw you a lifeline. They may have given you support or let you have a ride in their boat at a time when they were struggling themselves. These are the people to be thankful for, those who deserve your appreciation, and they should be praised for their part in your journey and encouraged to be with you in the future.

> *Anyone can be your friend when the sea is calm but only true friends stay with you during a storm.*

On the other hand, there may have been crew members or pirates who were only focused on themselves and their own needs. They may have taken advantage of the storm to try and sabotage you, or they might simply have ignored your plight. Should these people be allowed to continue as members of your crew? This is a decision only you can make, but even if you choose to continue your relationship with them, remember what colours they flew when things were hard.

Was a member of your crew responsible for the storm? If so, can you help them to see how their actions affected you and your journey? Even if they've apologised, can you trust them not to repeat their actions in the future?

Have the dynamics of any of your relationships changed? This can take time to get used to. If you don't like the way things have changed, tell the people involved – explain how you are feeling and why. No one can read your mind and they may not have realised how you feel about what has happened and how badly it may have affected you. A frank but friendly discussion might clear the air and make everyone feel better.

If the storms you endured were simply down to bad luck (accidents or other traumatic events), are you now scared of history repeating itself?

Perhaps you don't want to carry on with your journey in case another (maybe worse) storm arises?

That's a perfectly natural response after any storm, but these thoughts can be debilitating. Being fearful of the future could make you too scared to do anything. If you feel this is happening to you and it's affecting your well-being, seek help. Try talking to a trusted crew member, and if this doesn't work, seek help from a professional, such as a doctor or a counsellor. Don't ignore it.

Equally, after your storm has passed, if you still feel that you are drowning, get professional help as soon as possible.

All of us have been through storms in our past which, if we keep focusing on them, will hold us back. It is important to look forward and think of our future gains, and not our past losses, no matter how awful they were.

Perhaps the storm has cleared your vision?

When the dark clouds have shifted, maybe you can look at your life in a new light?

Sometimes, where things used to look and feel bleak, a storm can clear away old thoughts and make everything brighter.

Remember to be kind to yourself.

Take all the time you need to come to terms with changes, to accept or recoup any losses you've borne, and don't rush into big decisions.

If you're in doubt about what to do, if you feel like a fog bank has descended on you, simply sit in your boat and wait for things to become clear. Time truly is a great healer and as it passes, the mist will lift, and you'll be able to see ahead.

Don't try to rush this process.

Spend some time every day simply being thankful for everything you still have in your life. Be grateful for everything you can think of – your family and friends, your home, clothes, food, etc. Go for a walk and be grateful for the air you breathe, for the nature around you – birds flying, leaves on the trees, and any animals you encounter.

Concentrate on appreciating everything you have and try to avoid spending time dwelling on your losses.

What have you gained from the storms in your life?

Some of the changes our storms bring can be beneficial in the long-term, although it can be hard to see that from the centre of a maelstrom, or when you've just escaped from one.

As you look back on your life and all the storms you've survived to date, you should be able to see some positive things which you have gained from them. These can include:

- Thankfulness that the storm wasn't a lot worse than it was and that you (eventually) came out of it intact.
- A positive change in some, or all, of your attitudes.
- An increased physical or mental resilience.
- A better appreciation of your crew (the people around you) who helped you to get through the worst times.
- New skills that you can use to protect yourself in the future.
- The knowledge that everything changes and you can adapt to new circumstances.

- A new perspective on what is important to you as you continue along your chosen course.
- The ability to appreciate the small but valuable things in life.
- Patience (especially if you had to hang on for dear life and wait the storm out).

Remember that whatever you've survived in the past has helped to make you into the person you are today.

Just as the tides and waves on the ocean keep coming and going, you've bounced back, or at least ebbed and flowed along with them.

You are a survivor, even if you don't feel like one at this moment in time!

Having survived your storms, perhaps you now realise that you can cope better than you thought you could?

And now that the storm is over, let's talk about squaring up to future storms and better equipping yourself for them – even if you don't know what they will be yet. It's time to work on becoming more proactive and less reactive.

If you panic whenever something goes wrong, or even when you just think that something may go wrong, examine why. Where did the behaviour come from and what does it result in?

A calm approach to a storm will make it less scary. You can't always change an event, but you can always change your response to it.

You can make some preparations to help you to deal with the next storm that appears on the horizon.

'Expect the best but plan for the worst' is a good mantra.

To lessen the impact of your next storm, you may want to implement some or all of the following:

Health

Improving your health may help you to avoid future problems. Having your boat in the best possible seaworthy condition will help you to weather any future storms.

If you're overweight, try to lose a few pounds. If you know you smoke or drink too much, try cutting down. Take the time each day to eat a proper meal. Avoid just grabbing a snack, especially if you are dashing from one task to another. Plan your main meals for the week, factoring in plenty of fresh fruit and vegetables, so that you don't have to think about what you're going to eat.

Exercise is also key to maintaining your boat. This does not mean you have to join a gym or take up running or jogging. Simply going for a walk each day will help. There are numerous online classes you can join, too. Many are free, and no one can see you dancing or prancing around in your living room!

If, on the other hand, you live your life at a frantic pace, perhaps you should take some time out to relax. Yoga may not be for everyone, but a long soak in a hot bath (with no interruptions), listening to music, reading a book, watching your favourite TV program, and turning off phones or other distractions, can all help.

Take a look at your sleeping patterns. Would you benefit from going to bed a little earlier, investing in blackout curtains, or simply leaving electronic devices in another room?

If you've tried these things and you still have concerns about your health and well-being, as always, we suggest consulting your medical practitioner.

Emotions

Learning how to handle our emotions is useful. Practice staying calm. Deep breathing exercises are good for your body and mind. If you're faced with a storm in the future, you can fall back on this to stay focused and to cope better. There are many techniques to help you focus your mind; you just need to find the one that works for you.

If you react badly to the arrival of any storm, either by flapping about in a fear-filled panic, running away, or becoming paralysed, it won't do you or anyone else involved any good at all. Practice staying composed, not taking anything too personally, and not overreacting.

If you have issues with your emotional responses to hard times, get help. Talk to your GP or a counsellor, take an emotional management course, or join a support group.

Assess

Learning from your prior experiences, whether they were good or bad, will help you to prepare for whatever lies ahead.

Once you are calm, you can assess any approaching storms and consider what impact they may have on you and what you may be able to do about it. Decide what is under your control, and if there's something you can do to lessen the impact of the storm or make it go away, do it! It may be minor, but it's better than nothing.

Your Crew

'*A trouble shared is a trouble halved*,' so even if you're not sure they'll be able to help, roping your crew in is a good tactic! They may even have skills or expertise you're unaware of that will help you in the future.

Financial Difficulties

Money problems are one of the main storms people have to face.
If you've survived a financial storm but feel there could be more on the horizon, now is the time to develop a plan.

If you think it might be a short-term problem look at your finances and by making a few cutbacks, you may be able to avoid the storm. However, if the problem could be more serious the first thing to do is to speak to someone, don't be afraid to ask for help; avoid putting your head in the sand, hoping it will go away!

A starting point is to speak to your bank. They should be able to go through your income and outgoings to help you come up with a plan. Alternatively, there are a number of organisations where you can get free help and support from trained professionals who are paid to help you and not make money from you.

These organisations include:

Citizen's Advice	Tel. 0800 240 4420
Step Change Debt Charity	Tel. 0800 138 1111
National Debtline	Tel. 0808 808 4000

The sooner you can seek help the quicker you will be able to plan your way through the storm or even avoid it completely.

Whenever possible, try and save for that rainy day. When you can, put money aside in an emergency fund. Keep it in a separate place (preferably a bank or building society account and not in a box under your bed) where you can add to it but not access it too easily.

Look at the Long-Term

If you can't see any future through the storm, if all you can see is the lashing rain, thunder, lightning, and dark clouds rolling towards you, stop and ask yourself if it will have a long-term effect on you.

Will it be important in a week? A month? A year? Ten years? If not, there's no need to overreact.

If it's something that may have long-term consequences, work through what you think these will be, and then plan how to deal with them before the storm hits. Add to your current plan or compose a separate plan to deal with the upcoming storm and chart a route for navigating through it.

Looking back at your last storm and assessing how you coped may give you insights about yourself. If you can see that you didn't handle certain aspects well, that you could've done things better, examine what happened.

Look back without fear, anger, or shame; the past has gone and there's nothing you can do to change it now, but you can work on how you will behave when/if another storm hits.

It's time to believe in your ability to respond to things in the right way. You've been through storms before and survived; you can do it again.
If you're still a little uncertain about proceeding, take up your oars and start to row again, but go more slowly than you would have done before the storm.

What you do next is up to you.

This is your journey.

This is your life.

Whatever you decide to do next, you should congratulate yourself on getting as far as you have.

When John was safely back home with Pat, Sam took some time to reflect on what had happened and what he could have done differently. He knew that if somebody needed his help again, he would still offer assistance, but he would take more precautions – both for his own sake and for the sake of others.

Sam still had the issue of the colleague who said he had been irresponsible, but he soon realised that this colleague was not a true friend, so he decided he no longer had space or time for him in his life and cut all contact with him outside of work.

Not long after, a national lockdown was imposed once more, the hotel closed, and Sam was furloughed again.

Sam used the extra time to further develop his business ideas, and also worked to increase his conscious appreciation of many things he had previously taken for granted: he listened more closely to the birds singing while out with Bobby and kept in touch with his mum and friends via regular phone and video chats.

The brush with COVID-19 had been a stark reminder of the fragility of life and how much he had to live for.

He was determined to never again let his life revolve around working for someone else, and worked hard on his plan for after the pandemic. He decided that nothing was going to stop him from eventually reaching his destination.

By Christmas, Jo had learnt to appreciate a lot of the things she had previously taken for granted. Her family and friends had always been important to her, but Cassie's accident and the ongoing COVID-19 pandemic had also made Jo think about how life could be snatched away at any time. When she heard about Sam's brush with COVID-19, it only increased that sensation.

Being unable to help Cassie when she was in hospital had been horrible for Jo. She had felt almost overwhelmed by anger and fear. Being kept away from her injured child had rocked her world. It had left her feeling that she'd been selfish to try and take more time for her hobbies and interests, and had made her feel she should be devoting every waking second to her family.

With Cassie at home, the balance began to restore itself, and Jo was able to remember that while her family were the most important thing in her life, they weren't the only thing. Making time for herself and her own interests was equally important.

As Cassie recovered, the storm clouds cleared and the relief and gratitude Jo felt every day gave her a new sense of optimism. If nothing else, the thought that everything, no matter how bad it is at the time, eventually changes and passes, taught Jo a lesson and gave her comfort.

She was calmer, she and James were closer than ever, Jack would be coming home for the holidays, and Cassie was recovering well. Jo was very grateful that they had all survived the awful months which had ended 2020.

Sharon and Viv – Our Journey cont'd...

As our health storms began to recede and the sea became calm again, we put down our oars and took stock of what we had rowed through and where our future lay.

Viv – After the acute attack of sciatica, my symptoms began to ease, but progress was slow. Still, I was grateful that the worst was over and that my pain had subsided, and I became optimistic that it would continue to improve. Throughout this period, my emotions ebbed and flowed. Sleepless nights took their toll, as did the occasional flare-up. Luckily, those closest to me supported me through it.

Sharon – After a tense two weeks, the biopsy results came back negative, which was a major relief. However, it had not solved the problem and I still had an ugly growth on my face. After a routine blood test, the practice nurse offered some alternative treatments. I was pleased that somebody was showing an interest and was eager to try anything.

For weeks, I walked around with dressings on my face, as different treatments were tried. The hardest part was dealing with the stares and questioning looks of clients and members of the public. Thankfully, a treatment was found that worked, and I have only been left with a small scar, a reminder of the storm I survived.

We both developed a greater appreciation for where we were as opposed to where we could have been. We still had to be careful and follow the COVID-19 precautions to keep ourselves and our loved ones safe, but it could have been so much worse, and we were truly grateful it wasn't.

As the UK entered its third lockdown, we still had to communicate via video calls, emails, and phone.

In February 2021, we were both still working our day jobs, handling the pressures of being front-line key workers. Everyone we worked with was tired and tempers became frayed. Working through the pandemic with little to look forward to was taking its toll on us all.

The one glimmer of hope on the horizon was the roll-out of vaccines, together with the government's proposed route out of lockdown, with June being the target for lifting all restrictions.

Writing *Row Your Own Boat* and following our own course became even more important to us both. Neither of us were well off, so we continued to balance our jobs and work on the project together. In the short term, this was okay, but it soon became clear we could not continue to give 100% to everything, and there was a real worry that either our jobs, our health, or the project would suffer – storms neither of us wanted to row through.

After a particularly stressful period in our day jobs, we had both independently reached a point in our journey where we had to ask ourselves where we wanted to be, and what we wanted to do in the future.

Could we continue as we were, trying to balance all the demands on our time?

Should we finish the book, making that our single destination, but forgo our dream of developing the supporting website, training courses, etc., and everything that entailed?

To help us to decide, we wrote a detailed *Row Your Own Boat* business plan and itemised as many things as we could think of that we needed to do. Seeing how much work we still had to do to succeed, we independently came to the same conclusion; if we continued to work for others, it would take years to complete the project.

Should we turn back to the shore, moor our boats, and return to the easier lives we had before we started rowing our own boats, proud that we had at least tried to reach our destination?

OR

Should we take a leap of faith, do what we were encouraging our fellow rowers to do, and seize the opportunity to *Row Our Own Boat*?

We both had a few sleepless nights, each trying to decide what to do. Should we follow our heads or our hearts?

We both experienced waves of emotions, trepidation and apprehension, hope and optimism, combined with a great deal of soul searching.

We independently examined our financial situations, weighing up what the risks would be against the potential rewards.

We talked it over with our families, friends, and each other, but neither of us wanted to push the other into doing something they were not ready for.

Finally, however, we decided that we both believed in what we were trying to achieve, and we felt that if we didn't do it now, we would never do it.

This was our united decision:

YES, we were going to continue rowing our own boats to complete the book.

YES, we would develop the supporting website and training courses with the goal of helping our fellow rowers reach their destinations, so they could live the best life possible.

This in turn would enable us to live our BEST LIVES.

The only way we could truly commit 100% to reaching our destination was to take that final step and to leave our day jobs.

When we handed in our resignations, we again went through a roller-coaster of emotions. Most of our family and friends supported us and offers of networking opportunities began to come in (far more than we had anticipated).

A few people around us had concerns, however. It wasn't that they doubted our abilities, but they questioned whether this was the right time for this project, and if the financial risk would be too great. Would the pandemic hinder our progress?

We worked hard to set their fears to rest, with the hope that as time went by and we achieved each of our milestones, their concerns would be addressed.

Emotionally and financially, we needed to be open and honest with each other. We were scared. We had both made a life-changing decision, and the amount of work we still had to do to produce the quality of service we wanted to offer was daunting. However, once we had made the decision, we were even more excited that we were actually doing it and not just talking about it.

This was our time. It was our journey, and we were ready.

We were under no illusions and knew that we had a long and difficult journey ahead, especially as we were still under lockdown. There could be storms on the horizon, but rowing together, we would face whatever life threw at us and would do our best to come out the other side with even more determination to reach our destination.

We planned to enjoy every stage of the journey; every turn of our oars would be taking us closer to our goal.

We are now ***Rowing Our Own Boat*** full-time, and we hope that sharing our journey with you has motivated you to do the same.

> *When you have been through a storm and survived, never forget that although you were under the waves, you chose not to stay there.*

Chapter 9 – Reaching Your Destination

Row, row, row your boat,

See the water run,

Rowing here and rowing there,

Now your journey's done.

In this chapter we cover:

- Reaching your destination
- Evaluating your journey
- What comes next?

So, you've finished your journey and, hopefully, you've reached your chosen destination.

Now you can sit back, relax, and congratulate yourself on a job well done.

Or can you?

Before you step ashore to enjoy the results of all your hard rowing, take a moment to look around and ask yourself how you feel.

Was it worth it?

We hope so.

Is your new location where you wanted to be?

If the answer is a resounding *'YES!'* we would like to be the first to offer our congratulations and to say that we are so pleased for you and that we hope you're proud of everything you've accomplished along your journey.

Let's pause for a moment, though. If you've got to the destination you aimed for, but it's not quite what you expected, what can you do now?

In reality, perhaps your dream destination is not much better than where you were before.

Why?

What's wrong with where you are now?

Are you disappointed?

Do you feel that you've wasted all your time and effort?

If it feels like you've anchored your boat and all you've got on board is a load of ballast instead of the treasure you were searching for, what now?

Should you settle for where you are or consider whether you want (or need) to move on to something new?

What should or could you do next?

Remember Survivors' Shore from Chapter 2. This is where people who have worked hard and come a long way have got to – but it's not necessarily the end of their journey. They aren't at Success Point yet, and they may want to keep going.

If you aren't sure if you should stay where you are, take some time to yourself and think about the following questions. You don't have to give firm answers right now; simply consider your initial response when asked:

My Boat

How do I feel, physically and mentally?

Am I okay with my boat as it is now?

Is there anything I am unhappy with? Why, and how can I make it better?

Do I still have negative habits or thoughts that are holding me back?

Do I need to work on building new, empowering habits?

My Crew

How do I feel about my crew members?

Are they a positive or negative presence in my life?

Have they supported me or hindered my progress?

Who did I spend the most time with during my journey?

Who do I spend quality time with?

If I wanted to improve my relationships, have I managed it?

Do I feel that I've been too harsh to others or maybe even that I've left people behind who I should have kept close?

Do my close crew and other people around me treat me differently now?

Is that a good change or not (and does it bother me)?

My Journey

What have I gained from my journey?

Did I achieve or improve the things I wanted to? If not, why not?

If I achieved what I set out to do, am I living my dream? If not, why not?

Do I need to move on, change and/or improve anything else? If so, why?

If you're still not sure about your outcome, look back and remember where you were at the start of your journey.

Read the notes you made and remember how you used to feel. Think about the dreams, hopes, and wishes you had back then and compare them to where you are now. Gauge how far you've come.

If your goal was to master a new skill and you've made good progress towards it, appreciate what you have done.

Have you grown as a person?

Are you more confident, more self-assured, or more assertive?

Was progressing your career a major goal? Have you achieved a new role but found that it's just as stressful or even worse than your old position was?

How is your financial situation now? Better or worse?

If you're worse off financially but you're happier and more content in yourself, is that okay, or has it given you a whole new set of problems to work on?

If you decided to improve your diet, health, or fitness levels, where are you now?

Did you reach your targets?

Do you feel good about yourself?

Do you want (or need) to do more?

Is there anything you could have done differently?

Look back to when things weren't going so well in your life.

<u>Think about the differences between the beginning of your journey and where you are now</u>.

If you're not sure that where you are now is where you were hoping you'd be, if something in your life still feels *'off,'* now is the time to answer the following questions:

Am I the same person I was when I started my journey? Have I grown or changed? If so, in what ways? If not, why not?
What have I learned about myself and others along the way?
What have I achieved? (It doesn't matter how little or how slow you think your progress has been. List everything you can think of here.)

What new skills have I acquired?
What new or improved habits do I have now?
What would I still like to improve (what am I unhappy with)?
Do I need to plan another journey? If so, where to?

The process of development and growth can take longer than we expect. Some of us have to test and reject a few routes on different journeys until we feel happy with the results and the effect on our lives.

Remember not to look at others when assessing your potential or actual journeys. What they are doing doesn't matter. What you are doing is the only thing that's important. You should simply aim to feel better about yourself by following YOUR life's journey.

So, at this point, if you're not completely happy with your results, it's up to you, and you alone, what you decide to do next.

Coping with disappointment

If you are a little disappointed with where you've found yourself, own the feeling and move past it.

What you need to do now is to realise and acknowledge that life is about moving forward, about growing and experiencing different things, and that this point need not be the end of your journey.

You've probably learned a lot about yourself and your capabilities, so you don't need to criticise yourself or think that you did something wrong.

Appreciate what you've managed to do and be honest in your assessment of your journey.

Also, remember that no one else is entitled to criticise what you have done or where you've got to, so you can ignore any negative comments. This also applies to any internal comments you may be making; you know better than to criticise yourself, don't you?

Now is the time to look back over your journey and appreciate your achievements, no matter how small you believe they are. You've been on this voyage to improve yourself, or a certain aspect of your life, and even if you can only see a few minor improvements, you've made a brilliant go of it!

You set out to achieve something.

You looked at your life, planned what you wanted, and set off to find it.

Many people never, EVER go as far as you have gone.

You believed in yourself and took your life in hand by making changes (big or small) to live the only life you've been given in a better way.

Don't beat yourself up over anything that didn't quite work out the way you hoped.

So many people never closely examine their lives and never question the way they are living, let alone try to do anything to improve it. You should celebrate every victory you've had, no matter how small, and every single change you've made along the way.

Now you can look in the mirror and be proud of yourself, knowing that you won't have to live with regret for not trying to make things better or taking the chances you've taken.

Things may not be quite what you expected, but there's no shame in being where you are now. Everyone has colour in their pasts, and those who have taken big risks – even if those risks turned out to be wrong – are to be admired for taking the time to explore their possibilities and learn from their mistakes.

VALUES

At this point in your journey, it may be worth re-evaluating where you are and what's important to you.

Has your journey, and any storms you've been through, changed the way you value anything in your life?

Are some things more important to you now than they used to be?

Have you realised that some of the things (or people) you valued the most before you began your journey, no longer seem to be so important?

As you look at the list below, make a note of how your values have changed and why.

- Friends and family
- Health and well-being
- Time
- Honesty
- The future

Now ask yourself the following question –

Are you feeling happier, but still want more?

Perhaps you're happy with what you've learned or achieved, but you feel there's more you could do.

Maybe you enjoyed most (if not all) of the voyage and you are feeling more confident in your abilities.

Perhaps you're so pleased with yourself and enjoyed the process so much that you want to carry on exploring other oceans in your life's journey.

Do you want to add to your achievements?

You only have one life, so how do you want to spend the rest of it?

Each of us has so many options we can choose from:

- If you have lost some weight, is it time to improve your fitness levels?
- If you have mastered a new hobby, could you move on to an advanced level?
- If you have started a business venture, are you ready to expand it?
- If you have worked on your career or job role, do you have your sights set higher?

If you answered yes:

You can start this whole process again.

Simply plot a new course, get back in your boat, and set off on your next adventure!

You can add to your successes for as long as you feel the urge to achieve something else; you can *Row Your Own Boat* to any number of new destinations.

This is your boat, and you can continue your journey in any direction you choose.

For some of you, the desire to continue may spur you on to bigger and better things, but for others, you may feel that for now, this is where you need to be. Still, remember that at any time in the future, you can step back into your boat, pick up your oars, and start rowing again.

You now know that you're brave enough to try new things, so believe in yourself and do all the things you want to do.

Even if your journey to date has been a little bit disappointing, you can always:

Start again to make a new ending!

To do this, simply go back to Chapter 1, reassess your life from where you are now, and work towards any new or revised goals or desires you have.

You've got the knowledge and the ability, and you know that the possibilities for your life are boundless.

Seas the day!

CELEBRATE!

So right now, today, be happy and proud of what you've accomplished and everything you've learned during your voyage.

We hope you've enriched your life and that you can now stand tall and feel proud of yourself.

Your life is a gift to be made the most of, so you should enjoy it while you can and experience it to the full.

Wherever you are right now, whether you've reached your dream destination or not, we hope that you have all the tools you need to journey on and make your life even better.

Keep trying and eventually you will find a place
where you can drop anchor, be content,
and live life on your own terms.

The second lockdown ended on 2nd December, but Sam's area was put into Tier 3, meaning the hotel could not reopen. It was still closed when the third lockdown began in January 2021. Hotels were not expected to open again until at least 7th May, so Sam had plenty of time to think about his goals and what he'd achieved.

He was happy with his social life, as far as COVID-19 would allow, exercising outdoors with people and seeing his mum, who was in his support bubble. It wasn't what he wanted in the long-term, but he had plenty of plans for when COVID-19 was over.

Sam's goal of having a dog had been achieved through the dog share; he continued to walk Bobby every day. They both enjoyed the walks, and Sam felt that it was a double bonus because he was also helping his neighbours. John's bout of COVID-19 had left him out of breath and unable to walk long distances with a healthy dog.

Sam's main goal of having his own business was still on the horizon, despite the stalled start due to the lockdowns. He could not afford to stop working at the hotel, but he was determined to make some positive changes as soon as he could.

In March Sam spoke to his manager and asked if he could train two of his team to become assistant reception managers so that he could reduce his hours. He wrote a plan and sent it, complete with costs and savings, to the whole management team. They agreed to give Sam six months after reopening, lockdowns permitting, to prove it could work.

In May, when they re-opened, Sam agreed to return to work on a full-time basis for the first two months so that he could develop the new team, with a view that if everything went to plan, at the end of the trial, the trainees would be ready to take on their new roles and he could reduce his hours and get his new business up and running.

Sam was proud that he had had the nerve to put his recommendations to his bosses, but was even more amazed that he'd been given the go-ahead. Sam knew that for the first three months at least, it would be hard work. He would need to rewrite his business plan to allow for full-time work at the hotel, but his destination was in sight.

One afternoon, while watching Bobby playing with the other dogs in the park, Sam took some time to reflect on what had happened during the last few months. He was happier and healthier than he had been for a long time, and taking steps towards running his own business. He realised that even the simple task of taking Bobby on his walks had given him so much to be thankful for. He had made new friends of fellow dog walkers and now had a good network, even if they currently only met outside.

Some of them had suggestions and input for his business, and one or two had even offered him help. Sam had also met a dog walker named Sophie and her dog Molly and they went for walks together most days. They got on well together and agreed that when restrictions were lifted, they would go on trips out together. It was early days, but Sam was hopeful.

Sam occasionally met Jo for a walk or a picnic and shared his plans and progress with her. He knew he could rely on her to give him an honest opinion. All his friends had enjoyed his birthday 'party in a box', but he was still flattered when she asked if he could come up with some ideas for her parents' 50th anniversary in the summer. She was hoping that he would be able to book a venue, but if the pandemic was still raging, she needed other options and she was confident that he would be able to provide some alternatives.

Despite the pandemic, Sam knew he had a lot to be grateful for and that he would forge ahead with his plan as soon as possible. If things did not go as planned, he was confident that he could always start again.

As he thought about the previous months, Sam realised that some things were more important to him now than before the pandemic. He decided to write down his revised values and his thoughts for the future:

Sam's 2020/21 Values

Friends and family

I am closer to Mum and value my true friends (who I had neglected before COVID-19) more.

In the past, my personal relationships had suffered due to my long working hours. I won't make that mistake again.

Through walking Bobby, I've made friends with other dog walkers especially Sophie and Molly.

Health and well-being

Making time to exercise and eat regular healthy meals is something I now value and enjoy, along with walking Bobby.

I've been stressed out at times, but I've learned that I will survive, and come out of the other side stronger.

Time

2020/21 forced 'time' on me. Being furloughed allowed me to spend time thinking about my life, where I was, and where I wanted to be. It took a while to learn how to take time to stop and absorb what is around me, but I now really value this. It grounds me physically and gives me a sense of peace.

They say that 'Life is not a dress rehearsal'. I wish I had learnt this sooner and hadn't let work dictate my life for so long.

Honesty

Being honest with myself helped me to realise how much happier and healthier my life could be, and that it was down to me to do something about it!

The future

My goals are closer now and when I look back at the original lists and notes I made, I'm amazed at how far I've come and how prepared I am to deal with whatever lies ahead.

My 'party in a box' business will soon be up and running despite the lockdown, and the larger events side will follow when it becomes possible.

My future work-life balance will give me the freedom to enjoy my life and to start doing the things I want to do. I am grateful that I've had the time to get my life in order and plan a different future – something that wouldn't have happened if the pandemic hadn't forced my hand. I have hopes for a brighter future.

We only get one life and I want to live the rest of mine in the way I choose!

Jo's initial plan to change things and get a better life for herself had been a success and she felt that she had reconnected with the Jo she used to be before she became a wife and a mum.

She looked back at her original plan from the spring of 2020 and saw that she had achieved a lot of it:

1. *She had maintained her daily walk and exercised to online videos a couple of times a week.*
2. *She was better at saying 'no' to things she did not want to do.*
3. *The family meeting had gone well, and they all understood her needs and wishes.*
4. *James and his sisters were now caring for their parents, instead of expecting her to be responsible for them.*
5. *The new hobby she had wanted to find to use her creative skills was photography. She had finished the first part of her course and was looking forward to the next level. She was also hoping to go back to the animal shelter when the lockdown was over.*
6. *She and James had enjoyed regular date nights, even if it was a takeaway and a bottle of wine during the lockdowns.*
7. *She had used her journal to reflect on what she had achieved and the things she still felt she needed to work on.*

The only thing on her plan which she had not done was to write her bucket list, and that, she decided, would be the next thing she would do.

As she looked back over the last twelve months and reflected on how her life had changed since Sam first sent his lists for her to read, she was proud of the things she had achieved.

Before taking control, it had been easy to just live and 'go with the flow,' without questioning whether any of the things she was doing were what she wanted. She also realised that somewhere along the way, she had mistakenly come to believe that it would be selfish if she put her own needs before those of her family.

Identifying her goals, planning her course, and making the small but necessary changes had made a positive impact on everyone.

She began to think about the future.

What would she want to do when the pandemic was over?

When the kids were back at university or had left home, what did she want to be doing then?

What path should she follow for the next part of her journey through life?

Jo knew it was time to start again, time to write a new plan, with new ideas of what she could do next.

She now knew that anything could be possible with the right support, and a lot of planning and determination on her part.

Jo's 2020/21 Values

Friends and family

Spending quality time with those I love and valuing them is high on my list. Spending quality time with my family has helped me to re-connect with them all as individuals.

Talking to neighbours while out on my photography walks has helped me to develop a real sense of community spirit.

Health and well-being

I know that staying fit and well by exercising and eating sensibly will help me to face whatever lies ahead and give me the strength to help and support others.

I know I need to allow myself time to heal after facing anything major. I want to be strong for others, but I know I don't have to be, and that's fine.

Time

Spending quality time with my family and friends is precious but I now value taking some time for myself, to do things that give me joy, without feeling guilty.

I value taking time to be still and appreciate the things around me more. When photographing nature, I find that I see things better when I am calm and still.

2020/21 has taught me to value every moment of every day and take nothing for granted.

Honesty

Being honest with myself and recognising what I want from life has been invaluable.

The future

I value having the opportunity to try new things and widen my horizons. My photography has now given me a new hobby and the chance to help to raise money for charity, which could lead to new adventures.

Having the opportunity to go where I want to, when I want to, with anyone I want will never be taken for granted again!

Sharon and Viv – Our Journey cont'd ...

Our first destination of finishing the book, '*Row Your Own Boat'*, has been a success.

We are happy to have achieved what we originally planned, which was to produce a book that would hopefully inspire and encourage our readers to live their best lives.

Developing our website was by far the toughest, most demanding stage on our journey. Our vision for the site was clear, but getting it to a stage that we were happy with was a challenge, especially as neither of us were web designers, and we did not have a never-ending supply of funds to throw at it. Our course was replotted on several occasions as we learnt more about what we could and couldn't achieve on our site.

There were times when we wondered if we were doing the right thing, but our passion and belief in what we were hoping to achieve was all the motivation we needed to continue rowing our own boats.

The website will be an ever-evolving project as we continuously expand and improve on it, in our attempt to provide our fellow rowers with all that they need in a constantly changing world.

This also applies to our Instagram and Facebook pages. We will always be open to new ideas and suggestions from our rowers and will incorporate them whenever possible to enhance other rowers' future journeys.

We also hope that we will be able to include our rowers' success stories, along with their failures, to support and encourage their fellow rowers on their journeys, developing a community where all our rowers will flourish.

When we began our journey, where we are now was a far-off dream destination, but once our original goals were achieved, we realised that we still had so much more to give.

It has not been an easy journey, especially during the pandemic. We have laughed (boy, have we laughed) and at times we've cried. We've experienced every emotion you can think of at various stages through this journey together, but we would not have missed it for the world.

Just as the world has changed, our dreams have changed and evolved, but our main objective, to help and encourage our readers to live their best lives, remains the same.

Whenever new opportunities present themselves in the future, we've decided that we will be ready to adapt and evolve with them, especially if it will help our fellow rowers.

Sharon and Viv's 2020/21 Values List

If nothing else, living and working through a global pandemic has given us time to reassess our values and appreciate what we've missed out on.

We started working on this book during the COVID-19 pandemic (July 2020) and have faced many challenges along the way. Although we've both produced our individual 2020/21 values lists, below are the values we've explored while working our way through from the initial ideas to the completed book.

2020/21 – Working on *Row Your Own Boat* has taught us to value:

Family and friends

We both value family and friends more now than at the start of our voyage. Both of our families and all our friends have been supportive, and have cheered us on through every stage of our journey.

Health and well-being

As we have both had our share of health problems, now more than ever we value our health and the health of our loved ones. While facing the many storms the pandemic threw at us, we both learnt the value of taking time out to heal.

Time

The COVID-19 pandemic and lockdowns were hard on everybody and for a while, we both struggled to battle the storm, but we now value the quality time we can spend working together, as opposed to video and telephone calls. We have also come to value how quickly time can fly, and how vital it is to make the most of every day.

Honesty

At the start of our *Row Your Own Boat* journey we agreed that we would be honest with each other, and this is a value which is as strong today as it was then.

Being honest both to ourselves and with each other, has helped us to stay focused on our goals as well as our hopes for the future.

We also learnt to value admitting when we were struggling so that we could help and support each other.

The future

The pandemic taught us to value our freedom and we will never take that for granted again.

Writing the book and producing and developing our website and training courses has also provided us with the freedom of working for ourselves both now and in the future.

As we come out of the pandemic, many people may be looking for something new in their lives, and if we can help them, we will have achieved our goal.

Chapter 10 – Final Words

Row, row, row your boat,

Gently down the stream,

Maybe next time, fool them all,

Become a submarine!

So, this is the last chapter in the book.

We hope you've enjoyed the process of working through this book, that you've picked up a few helpful thoughts and ideas, and that you've made some positive changes to your life along the way.

As we've said throughout the book, if you want to start again or need help to maintain your boat as you traverse this ocean of life, you needn't be alone on your journey.

You can reach out and join us and fellow travellers at www.rowyourownboat.co.uk, where we offer a range of support and training courses.

You can also find us on our @rowyourownboat21 Facebook page, or you can follow us at rowyourownboatonline on Instagram.

We would love it if you would share your successes with us and your fellow rowers who are out on the sea of life. Who knows – you could be an inspiration to many!

Equally, if you feel that you've not been particularly successful, we are sure that our community of rowers will offer help and support to get you back on course, so don't be shy; reach out!

We believe in you, and we hope that you now believe in yourself too.

At the start of your journey, we discussed the fact that contentment doesn't just happen. Most of us need to work for it.

We need to define what we think our contentment will look like and then work hard to make it a reality.

Yes, there are times when something we thought would make us happy didn't, but on the whole, we have the power to define our happiness and then work towards it.

Plus, we always have the option of starting again.

So, set yourself new targets and never stop trying to do what you need to do to make your life better.

In 2005, researchers Sonja Lyubomirsky, Kennon M. Sheldon, and David Schkade established that things like your financial status, your possessions, and your physical appearance only account for about 10% of your happiness and contentment.

A lot of people place a much higher value on lifelong learning, artistic activities and meaningful relationships. It's these things that enrich our lives. These are the people who actively pursue learning, try different hobbies, hone their skills, and are open to exploring new horizons.

The happiest, most contented people don't sit around waiting for the good things in life to come along; they go out and look for them.

Happy people can be seen enthusiastically looking for new ways to understand others. They seek out genuine friendships with like-minded people and constantly find techniques to fill their lives with contentment and peace.

They know they will not achieve sustained happiness by waiting for it to come to them – they go out, row their own boats, and find it. You can too.

We hope your life is now closer to being exactly what you'd like it to be, but that this is not the end of your journey.

It may have been just the first stage of your voyage and we hope that you've been motivated to go on to bigger and better things, with a new outlook on life and new destinations in sight.

If you haven't already done so, please join us on our *Row Your Own Boat* website, Facebook community and Instagram so we can share our journeys.

A final note from Viv

I spent many years collecting thoughts and noting ideas for this book and a long time dreaming about writing it, but I never had the courage to jump in my boat and head off on the journey to make it happen on my own.

Luckily, when I shared my 'Row Your Own Boat' thoughts with Sharon and asked if she'd like to join me on this journey, she embraced the dream with me.

I could not have imagined a better crewmate!

Working together, we assessed our skills, planned our voyage, stepped into our boats, and began to row on what has become the most fantastic, shared journey.

Despite battling through fierce storms, we have arrived at our first destination, finishing this book, satisfied that we've done our best.

We now hope to continue our work to help people to improve their lives in as many ways as possible. We are in our boats and will not be sitting at the quayside wishing our lives away – we will be out there rowing to do as much as we can to help as many people as possible.

We sincerely hope that as you have worked through this book, you have moved closer to your dreams, whatever they may be.

We also hope you have realised at least some of your wishes, that you've enjoyed the process, and that you are content in the knowledge that you've done what you wanted to do, or that you have tried your best (if you're not quite there yet).

Row, row, row your boat,

May all your dreams come true,

Contentment, health and happiness,

Is what we wish for you!

Row Your Own Boat

Are you keen to continue rowing your own boat to a happier and more contented life?

If the answer is "Yes", then please join our

Row Your Own Boat Online Community

www.rowyourownboat.co.uk

Completing this book was the first milestone on our Row Your Own Boat journey, the second being the development of our website and online community.

Our vision for this community is to provide a platform for our rowers to come together and to help and support each other on their row your own boat voyage.

We want to share our knowledge and experiences but, more importantly, provide our community of rowers with what is useful for them, based on their feedback and ideas.

As our community grows we will offer a variety of courses to support you and help you on your way. These include areas such as job search and assertiveness, all designed for any of our rowers to follow at their own pace.

We will also be introducing support groups where we can look at specific areas such as health and fitness, bereavement, and personal development.

Every month we will send out a newsletter to our members keeping them up to date with forth-coming events such as Facebook Live sessions including guest speakers, Q & A sessions and follow-on course workshops.

We do not claim to be experts in every area or subject, we are good, but not that good, but if we and our community cannot help, we will do our best to point you in the right direction.

We hope you will join our community and we can all support each other as we work towards our "Best Life"!

Sharon & Viv

Row Your Own Boat

Keep in touch with

Sharon Cleveley & Viv Walker

We love to connect with our readers on social media.

Find us on:

Facebook: @rowyourownboat21

Instagram: rowyourownboatonline

Row Your Own Boat

Printed in Great Britain
by Amazon

74507041R00119